The Forager's Harvest Bible

The Ultimate Guide to Identifying, Harvesting, Preparing and Storing Wild Products

By William Belle

The following book is provided below with the aim of delivering information that is as precise and dependable as possible. However, purchasing this book implies an acknowledgment that both the publisher and the author are not experts in the discussed topics, and any recommendations or suggestions contained herein are solely for entertainment purposes. It is advised that professionals be consulted as needed before acting on any endorsed actions.

This statement is considered fair and valid by both the American Bar Association and the Committee of Publishers Association, and it holds legal binding throughout the United States.

Moreover, any transmission, duplication, or reproduction of this work, including specific information, will be deemed an illegal act, regardless of whether it is done electronically or in print. This includes creating secondary or tertiary copies of the work or recorded copies, which are only allowed with the express written consent from the Publisher. All additional rights are reserved.

The information in the following pages is generally considered to be a truthful and accurate account of facts. As such, any negligence, use, or misuse of the information by the reader will result in actions falling solely under their responsibility. There are no scenarios in which the publisher or the original author can be held liable for any difficulties or damages that may occur after undertaking the information described herein.

Additionally, the information in the following pages is intended solely for informational purposes and should be considered as such. As fitting its nature, it is presented without assurance regarding its prolonged validity or interim quality. Mention of trademarks is done without written consent and should not be construed as an endorsement from the trademark holder.

Please note that even though this version has been paraphrased, it is still recommended to consult with a legal professional to ensure that the copyright adequately protects your rights and is compliant with the laws of your jurisdiction.

Table Of Content

Chapter 1
Introduction

Welcome to "The Forager's Harvest Bible: The Ultimate Guide to Identifying, Harvesting, Preparing, and Storing Wild Products." My aim is to equip you, the adventurer, the nature lover, the budding forager, with the knowledge and tools necessary to confidently embark on your foraging journey. We will explore the fascinating world of wild edibles and equip you with practical skills and information that you can directly apply in your daily life, all while preserving the integrity of the ecosystems we love.

I'm excited to share this knowledge with you. Whether you're an environmental scientist, an outdoor educator, a seasoned hobbyist forager, or a curious novice, this book is designed for you. The diverse range of topics covered in this guide aims to address your goals, challenges, and interests, ensuring a comprehensive and useful resource for your foraging journey.

The incredible diversity and richness of the natural world is truly awe-inspiring. It provides a vast array of wild products for us to discover, appreciate, and utilize. Yet, the art of foraging goes beyond merely finding food. It's about fostering a profound connection with nature, promoting sustainability, and realizing our role in preserving the environment for future generations.

Our journey will begin with exploring the philosophy and benefits of foraging, focusing not only on the health and sustainability aspects but also on the deep connection foraging allows us to establish with nature. We will also discuss the ethical considerations of foraging to ensure that we are respectful and sustainable in our practices.

Getting started, we'll discuss essential tools, basic safety guidelines, and the legal aspects of foraging. You'll become familiar with everything you need to know before you step foot in the wild.

Identifying wild edibles is one of the most critical aspects of foraging. You'll learn to understand plant structures, identify common edible plants, and distinguish them from dangerous lookalikes.

From there, we will delve into harvesting techniques, including when to harvest for optimal quality and how to do so without harming the plant. Preparation of your foraged finds will then be covered, from cleaning to cooking, and understanding the nutritional value of your harvest.

Next, we'll cover the preservation and storage of wild edibles, touching on drying, canning, freezing, and other techniques that will allow you to enjoy your harvest long after you've returned from the field.

The latter part of the book is dedicated to advanced topics such as seasonal and habitat-specific foraging, foraging for medicinal plants, and other useful wild products. We'll share personal experiences, interviews with experienced foragers, and resources for further learning. A comprehensive glossary, quick identification guide, and a seasonal foraging calendar will serve as quick and practical references.

As we venture into the world of foraging together, rest assured, the information in this guide is detailed, reliable, and includes colorful, clear images to help you accurately identify plants. I understand that ensuring the safety and sustainability of your foraging practices is a primary concern. That's why every effort has been made to ensure that the descriptions, instructions, and safety guidelines are comprehensive and easy to understand.

Remember, foraging is more than a hobby or a pastime; it is a way to connect with nature and learn about the abundance it provides. So, grab your gear, open your mind, and let's embark on this wonderful journey together.

And now, let's move on to our first chapter, where we will begin our exploration into the philosophy of foraging.

The Philosophy of Foraging

As we set foot into the vast world of foraging, let's pause for a moment to contemplate the philosophical underpinnings of this practice. Foraging is not just a hobby or a means to procure food; it's an approach to life, a perspective that combines reverence for nature with our basic human needs.

At its core, the philosophy of foraging is about harmony—between humans and nature, between need and availability, between taking and giving back. As foragers, we tread the thin line of this balance with every plant we pick and every trail we follow. Our goal isn't simply to extract resources from the environment, but rather to interact with it in a manner that is respectful, sustainable, and deeply enriching.

Foraging invites us to be active participants in the intricate web of life. As we search for wild edibles, we become more attuned to the nuances of the natural world, more aware of the cycles and patterns that govern life around us. We begin to see how different organisms interact, how they contribute to their ecosystems, and how they adapt to changes in their environment.

Through this newfound awareness, we come to understand that we are not mere observers or consumers of nature—we are part of it. We play a role in shaping the world around us, just as it shapes us. This realization can be both empowering and humbling. It inspires us to interact with our environment responsibly, ensuring that our foraging practices contribute positively to the ecosystems we rely on.

Foraging also underscores the idea of resourcefulness. It prompts us to make the most of what nature freely offers us, rather than seeking artificial alternatives. This can be as simple as picking wild berries for a snack during a hike, or as complex as recognizing and utilizing an array of plants for medicinal purposes. The more we learn about the wealth of resources available to us in the wild, the more self-sufficient we become.

Yet, foraging isn't just about survival or self-sufficiency—it's also about delight and appreciation. There's a profound sense of joy that comes from finding, identifying, and harvesting wild edibles. This joy is not merely the result of the "hunt" or the prospect of a free meal—it stems from the deep connection we establish with nature through the act of foraging. We start to see the environment not just as a backdrop to our lives, but as a living, breathing entity filled with mysteries and gifts waiting to be discovered.

In essence, the philosophy of foraging is about mindfulness. It encourages us to be present, to truly see, touch, smell, and taste the world around us. It invites us to slow down, to pay attention to details we might otherwise overlook, to appreciate the simple yet profound acts of growth, survival, and renewal taking place all around us.

Moreover, it teaches us about resilience. Plants, especially those growing wild, are testaments to the power of life to persist under all sorts of conditions. Observing how these plants thrive—sometimes against all odds—can inspire us to adopt a similar resilience in our own lives.

Finally, foraging promotes the idea of stewardship. As we come to value and depend on the resources offered by our natural surroundings, we also feel a stronger responsibility towards preserving these resources. We understand that true sustainability doesn't lie in simply taking from nature, but in giving back to it, in ensuring that our practices support the health and diversity of our ecosystems.

By adopting a foraging mindset, we can transform our relationship with the natural world. We move from a paradigm of domination and exploitation to one of respect, gratitude, and reciprocity. We start to see ourselves as integral parts of the environment, bound to it by the simple yet profound act of eating.

In the following sections, we'll delve deeper into the benefits of adopting this philosophy in our lives—not just in terms of physical health and sustainability, but also in terms of the mental and emotional enrichment that comes from forming a deep, personal connection with nature.

As we embark on this journey, remember that foraging isn't just about what we gather—it's about what we learn, how we grow, and the way we perceive and interact with the world around us. It's about slowing down, paying attention, and embracing the beauty and abundance of the natural world.

We have much to learn, and much to discover. The path is laid out before us. All we need to do is take the first step.

The Benefits of Foraging: Health, Sustainability, and Connection

Let's unravel the numerous benefits it brings to our lives, touching upon our health, our environment, and our connection with nature. This practice isn't just about filling our baskets with wild edibles; it's about filling our lives with richness, awareness, and sustainability.

Health Benefits

Foraging for wild foods has significant health benefits. Wild plants often contain a plethora of nutrients, vitamins, and minerals, making them a powerhouse of nutrition. For instance, wild greens such as dandelion and nettle leaves can be rich in calcium, iron, and vitamins A, C, and K. Wild berries are typically packed with antioxidants, supporting our immune system and helping ward off diseases.

Wild foods also offer a diverse range of flavors and textures, which can invigorate our palates and inspire culinary creativity. Think of the tartness of wild blackberries, the delicate sweetness of violets, or the earthy taste of wild mushrooms.

Moreover, the physical activity involved in foraging—walking, bending, stretching, and occasionally climbing or crawling—provides an excellent form of exercise. It's a wonderful way to keep fit while enjoying the beauty and serenity of the outdoors.

Sustainability

Foraging promotes sustainability by encouraging us to rely on locally available, seasonally appropriate foods. This reduces our dependency on industrially produced and transported goods, which contribute significantly to carbon emissions.

Additionally, many wild plants are hardy and resilient, thriving without the need for chemical fertilizers or pesticides. By foraging, we're choosing food sources that are not only healthier for us, but also healthier for our environment.

However, sustainability in foraging also means practicing it responsibly. It involves harvesting in a manner that ensures the continued growth and propagation of plant species, and it requires an understanding of local ecosystems and their conservation needs. We'll explore these topics more in-depth in a later section.

Connection with Nature

Beyond the physical health and environmental benefits, foraging fosters a profound connection with nature. As we become skilled in identifying and harvesting wild edibles, we develop a greater awareness and appreciation of the natural world around us.

This connection isn't one-sided. Just as we learn to read nature—its cycles, its patterns, its language—nature, in turn, reads us. It reflects our impact on the environment, reminds us of our responsibilities as stewards, and often mirrors the health of our societies.

Through foraging, we come to understand that we're not separate from nature, but an intrinsic part of it. This realization often brings about a transformation in how we perceive and interact with our environment.

Furthermore, can strengthen our connection with our ancestors. It links us to age-old practices and wisdom, making us feel part of a lineage that stretches back to the earliest human societies. It can also deepen our sense of community as we share our knowledge, experiences, and foraged foods with others.

In sum, the benefits of foraging extend far beyond the physical act of gathering wild foods. It's a practice that nourishes our bodies, reduces our environmental impact, and cultivates a deep, meaningful bond with the natural world.

Principles of Sustainable and Respectful Foraging

Immersing ourselves in the act of foraging, we become part of the ecosystem around us. We step into a world of symbiotic relationships, delicate balances, and intricate growth patterns. As we fill our baskets with wild edibles, it becomes paramount to remember that we are not mere spectators or extractors. We are participants and caretakers. This sense of responsibility forms the foundation of ethical foraging, a topic we'll delve into now.

The principles of ethical foraging revolve around sustainability, respect for nature, and sharing knowledge. Let's unravel each one of these principles, exploring their meaning and implications in depth.

Sustainability

Sustainability, in the context of foraging, means harvesting in a manner that ensures the continued growth and propagation of plant species. It also signifies respecting the roles that these plants play within their ecosystems.

A sustainable forager only harvests what they need, leaving enough plants for wildlife, and for the plant population to replenish itself. It's a good rule of thumb to take no more than a third of the plants in a particular area. This rule, however, is not absolute. For some vulnerable species, even this might be too much.

Knowing when to harvest is also crucial for sustainability. Different plant parts— leaves, flowers, fruits, roots—should be harvested at specific times to minimize harm to the plant and to maximize nutritional and medicinal benefits. We'll discuss more on the timing of harvest in a later section.

Respect for Nature

Respect for nature is another cornerstone of ethical foraging. It involves recognizing the inherent worth of all living beings and treating them with reverence.

An ethical forager avoids trampling on plants, compacting soils, or causing undue harm to habitats. If a plant is flowering or seeding, the forager often leaves it alone to complete its reproductive cycle. If a plant is rare or endangered, the forager avoids harvesting it altogether.

Respect for nature also means complying with local laws and regulations related to foraging. Some areas might be protected or have restrictions on what can be harvested and in what quantities. Respect involves obtaining any necessary permits and adhering to the guidelines they stipulate.

Sharing Knowledge

The third principle of ethical foraging involves sharing knowledge. As foragers, we are privy to a wealth of information about nature, gathered through direct experience and observation. Sharing this knowledge with others helps promote responsible foraging practices and nurtures a wider appreciation for the natural world.

However, sharing knowledge must be done with caution. Misinformation can lead to the misidentification of plants, potentially resulting in harm to both people and plant populations. Hence, it's vital to ensure the accuracy of the information we share and to encourage others to cross-verify from reliable sources.

In conclusion, the ethos of ethical foraging is not merely about what we take from nature, but also about what we give back. It's about fostering a relationship with nature that is reciprocal, mindful, and imbued with a sense of stewardship. As we forge ahead on our foraging journey, let these principles guide us, ensuring that our harvests are bountiful not just for us, but also for the generations to come, and for the ecosystems that sustain us all.

Chapter 2
Getting Started: Tools and Safety

As we journey into the heart of the wild, preparedness becomes our best companion. It equips us with confidence, enhances our efficiency, and most importantly, safeguards our well-being. This chapter, is designed to set you on your foraging path with a well-stocked arsenal of knowledge and guidance.

We'll start by introducing the essential tools for foraging. You might already have some of these at your disposal, and others you'll learn are worth investing in. Whether it's a durable pair of gloves, a keen-edged knife, or a sturdy basket, each tool plays a pivotal role in making your foraging expeditions more fruitful and enjoyable.

However, tools alone don't make the forager. It's the careful attention to safety that transforms an outdoor enthusiast into a responsible forager. This is why we've dedicated a section to discuss the basic first aid and precautions necessary to avoid hazardous areas. Remember, the best foragers are those who not only know how to reap nature's bounty but also how to do it safely and responsibly.

Finally, we'll delve into the legalities and permissions related to foraging. Many foragers, particularly those new to this practice, are unaware of the regulations governing their activities. By shedding light on these aspects, we aim to foster a community of foragers who respect private property, protect natural reserves, and adhere to the laws of the land.

So let's venture forth. Your toolkit is waiting to be assembled, the safety measures are ready to be learned, and the nuances of foraging legally are ready to be unveiled.

Essential Foraging Tools: What You Need and Why

Just as a painter needs their brushes and a carpenter their tools, a forager too requires certain implements to make the most of their foraging experience. The tools that a forager carries help facilitate the identification, harvesting, and storage of wild products, all while minimizing the impact on the ecosystem. This section provides an extensive list of the essential tools you need, and more importantly, why each one has its unique place in a forager's arsenal.

The Forager's Toolkit

To begin, let's look at the must-have tools for any forager:

A Quality Field Guide: This is your first and most essential tool. Having a well-detailed guidebook, complete with colored images and precise descriptions of various plants and their parts, can make the difference between a fruitful day of foraging and a potentially dangerous misidentification. Choose a guide that is tailored to your local region for the best results.

A Notebook and Pen: These simple tools can become your best allies on your foraging trips. Jotting down your observations, sketching unfamiliar plants, or simply making a note of where you found a particular plant species can be immensely beneficial. It's the beginning of your personal foraging guide, tailored entirely to your experiences.

A Sturdy Basket or Bag: As you wander through the forests, meadows, or by the riverside, you'll need something to hold your bounty. A good quality basket or a bag is essential for carrying your finds. Baskets, in particular, are great as they allow air circulation, which can help keep your finds fresh longer.

A Foraging Knife: A compact, sharp knife is a crucial tool for any forager. It will be useful for cutting stems, digging up roots, or even opening nuts and shells. Consider one with a folding blade for easy and safe portability.

Gardening Gloves: Some plants can be prickly, others might have sap that can cause skin irritation. A robust pair of gloves can protect your hands while you are busy foraging.

A Trowel or Hand Shovel: These come in handy when you are trying to dig up roots or tubers without damaging them or the surrounding plants.

A Mesh Bag: A smaller mesh bag is great for collecting seeds or nuts. The holes allow for dirt and other debris to fall away, keeping your collection cleaner.

Clear Containers or Bags: These are useful for separating different types of foraged items, particularly when you are trying to keep fruits or vegetables separate from other foraged items.

A Camera: While not absolutely essential, carrying a digital camera or using the one on your smartphone can be a lifesaver when it comes to identifying plants. You can take a picture and compare it with your guide or consult an expert later.

A Magnifying Glass: This is a great tool to help you see the small details on plants that can be vital for correct identification.

Water Bottle and Snacks: Foraging can be hard work, and it's essential to stay hydrated and fueled. Always carry water and some energy-rich snacks with you.

Selecting the Right Tools

Now that we have a comprehensive list of tools, it's important to remember that the key to choosing the right tools lies in understanding your needs, preferences, and the specific demands of the areas you'll be exploring. Not all foraging expeditions will require all these tools. For instance, a simple trip to a known area might only require a basket, while an exploratory trip to a new location might necessitate the full arsenal.

Further, select tools that match your level of comfort and expertise. If you're just beginning your foraging journey, start with the basics: a reliable field guide, a sturdy basket, a pair of gloves, and a good knife. As your skills and interests expand, so too can your collection of tools.

Finally, while purchasing tools, give attention to their quality. Remember, these are investments in your foraging journey. A good-quality, well-maintained tool not only performs better but also lasts longer.

In conclusion, having the right tools is an integral part of the foraging process. They provide you with the means to effectively and safely find, collect, and transport your foraged finds. Equally important is the knowledge of why each tool is used, as it enables you to adapt your toolkit to various situations, enhancing your overall foraging experience.

Safety First: Basic First Aid and Avoiding Hazardous Areas

Safety, as they say, should never be an afterthought. Whether you're an experienced outdoorsman or a budding forager, understanding and adhering to safety guidelines is crucial. In this section, we'll delve into some basic first aid knowledge and tips on how to avoid potentially hazardous areas. This isn't merely about ensuring a safe return from your foraging adventures; it's also about empowering you with the confidence to explore the wilds more freely and respectfully.

Preparation: The First Line of Defense

Before setting foot in the great outdoors, it's paramount to prepare thoroughly. Apart from knowing what you're looking for and how to identify it, you should have a comprehensive understanding of potential dangers and how to avoid them. Equip yourself with suitable clothing and footwear, protective gear, and a first aid kit tailored to the outdoors.

Knowing the terrain and the environment is essential. Familiarize yourself with the area you plan to forage in—know its fauna, weather patterns, and the location of trails and landmarks. Knowledge is power, and in the wild, it can also be a lifesaver.

Basic First Aid Skills: Your Toolkit for Emergencies

Accidents can happen even in the most benign situations. A slight misstep can lead to a sprained ankle, or a hidden plant can cause a skin rash. Hence, knowing basic first aid skills is essential. Here are a few things that every forager should know:

Wound Care: Understand how to clean a wound, apply antiseptic, and bandage it properly. This can prevent infections and speed up healing.

Treating Sprains and Breaks: Learning how to immobilize a sprain or a break can prevent further injury and provide temporary relief before medical help arrives.

Heat Exhaustion and Dehydration: Recognize the signs of heat exhaustion and dehydration, and know how to treat them. Often, rest, shade, and hydration can quickly alleviate these conditions.

Hypothermia and Frostbite: In cold weather, knowing how to prevent and treat hypothermia and frostbite is crucial. Layering clothing, staying dry, and having a way to start a fire are key.

Avoiding Hazardous Areas

Not all parts of the wild are friendly or accessible. Certain areas could be hazardous due to steep terrain, dense undergrowth, poor visibility, or the presence of dangerous animals. It's crucial to recognize these dangers and steer clear of such areas. Here are a few tips:

Recognize Unsafe Terrain: Stay away from unstable or slippery slopes, cliff edges, and areas prone to landslides or falling rocks. Remember, your safety is more important than any foraging find.

Beware of Water Hazards: Rivers and bodies of water can pose risks. Be mindful of strong currents, sudden drops, and slippery rocks. If you're near the coast, be aware of the tide times.

Dangerous Animals and Insects: Some areas may be home to dangerous animals or insects. Learn about local wildlife, know how to avoid attracting or provoking them, and understand what to do if you encounter one.

Human-made Hazards: Be cautious around old buildings, fences, or machinery that might be hidden in overgrown areas. Also, be aware that some areas may be private property, have restricted access, or be subject to different rules and regulations.

Safe foraging is a craft that develops over time, balancing the thrill of discovery with the wisdom of caution. As you spend more time in nature, you'll learn to read the landscape and its subtle cues better. By prioritizing safety, you ensure that every foraging trip is a successful one, bringing you back home with a basket full of wild goodies and a heart full of memories.

Legalities and Permissions

Respecting Private Property and Protected Areas

Respecting the law and the rights of others is an important aspect of foraging, and this often involves understanding local regulations about harvesting plants, as well as obtaining appropriate permissions when necessary. Foraging is not a free-for-all; it is a privilege that comes with responsibilities. Let's explore some of these key legal and ethical considerations.

Understanding Local Regulations

Different jurisdictions have different laws regarding foraging. Some places, such as national forests in the U.S., often permit foraging for personal use. However, other areas like national parks and nature reserves may strictly prohibit it to protect the ecosystem. The regulations can also differ depending on the type of plant or animal product you're after – mushroom foraging, for instance, might have different rules than berry picking or hunting game.

To avoid legal troubles and contribute to the sustainable management of local ecosystems, it's crucial to familiarize yourself with these laws before heading out. Resources like local government websites, community foraging groups, or park ranger offices can provide valuable information.

Respecting Private Property

It's also essential to respect private property while foraging. If you come across a patch of edible plants on someone's land, always seek permission from the landowner before harvesting. Some landowners might welcome foragers, especially if they're aware of the mutual benefits – foragers get their harvest, while the landowners get free weed management.

Protecting Protected Species

Another important legal consideration is that some plant and animal species are protected by law due to their endangered or threatened status. These species are off-limits for foragers. Harvesting them can lead to serious legal consequences and contribute to the decline of the species. By being a responsible forager, you can play a part in the conservation of these vulnerable species.

Take Only What You Need

Lastly, a fundamental principle of ethical foraging is to take only what you need. Overharvesting can lead to a decline in plant populations and disrupt the balance of the ecosystem. As a rule of thumb, never take more than 10-20% of the plants in a given patch and always leave enough for wildlife, which may rely on the same plants for their survival.

In essence, foraging legally and ethically is about respect – respect for the law, for other people, and for the natural world. It's about being aware of the impacts of our actions and making conscious decisions that support the health and integrity of our ecosystems.

Chapter 3
Identifying Wild Edibles

Nature is a vast storehouse of edible bounty, waiting for us to discover. Walking through the woods or fields, you might be surprised by the variety of plants that can provide sustenance and flavors to our meals. But for every safe and edible plant out there, there could be another that looks similar but is harmful or even deadly. This is why the skill of correctly identifying wild edibles is a cornerstone of foraging.

In this chapter, we will delve into the details of how to accurately and confidently identify the bounty nature offers us. This chapter is designed to provide you with a comprehensive understanding of plant anatomy, specific profiles of common edible plants, and strategies to distinguish these edibles from their potentially dangerous lookalikes. Our aim is to equip you with the skills and knowledge that will empower you to safely forage on your own.

The journey of identifying wild edibles involves a blend of scientific understanding, careful observation, and a deep respect for nature. The more you practice, the more intimate you become with the unique character and beauty of each plant. Soon, you'll start to see the world around you with new eyes, recognizing the potential for a delicious meal where others see only a field of weeds.

Now, let's explore the wonderful world of wild edibles!

Plant Anatomy 101: Understanding Plant Structures

One of the most significant steps in becoming an effective forager is understanding the intricate world of plant anatomy. To the untrained eye, plants might just seem like a green blur of leaves and stems, but in reality, they are fascinating organisms with a complex structure and function. Identifying a plant is not about merely recognizing its leaf shape or color. It is about understanding how different plant parts — the roots, stem, leaves, flowers, seeds — interact with each other and their environment. So, let's dive deeper into the basic structure of plants and equip you with the knowledge to identify wild edibles accurately.

Roots: We start from the ground up, with the part of the plant that often lies unseen beneath the soil. Roots play a crucial role in a plant's survival. They absorb water and nutrients, anchor the plant to the ground, and sometimes, store food. There are many types of roots like the taproot (carrot, dandelion), fibrous roots (grass), adventitious roots (ivy), and more. Each of these types can give clues about the plant's identity. Some edible plants, like the burdock and chicory, have taproots that are used in various cuisines.

Stem: Moving upwards from the roots, we have the plant's stem. The stem provides support, helps transport substances between the roots and leaves, and also stores food. Stems can be herbaceous (soft, green) like in the case of spinach or woody like in trees and shrubs. They can stand erect or trail on the ground. The arrangement of leaves on the stem, called the leaf arrangement, is another key identifier. Plants can have alternate, opposite, or whorled leaf arrangements.

For example, Stinging Nettles, a popular wild edible, have opposite leaf arrangements, and the stem is square. On the other hand, the garlic mustard plant, another delicious wild edible, has alternate leaf arrangements.

Leaves: Leaves are the life force of the plant, responsible for photosynthesis. A plant's leaves can provide many clues for identification. Leaf shape, margin, and the pattern of veins are all crucial for identifying plants.

Consider the dandelion, an easily recognizable wild edible. Its leaves are deeply lobed with a unique tooth-like pattern on the margin, hence its French name 'dents de lion', meaning 'teeth of the lion'. Another example is the common plantain, a plant widely used in herbal medicine. It has broad, oval leaves with parallel veins running through them.

Flowers and Fruits: Flowers, apart from their aesthetic appeal, are a critical part of plant reproduction. The color, shape, size, and arrangement of flowers can all provide significant clues to a plant's identity. The number of petals, the form of the flower head (like the composite flowers of dandelions), and the time of blooming are all important details.

Take, for instance, the wild garlic, also known as ramps. Its flowers are white and umbrella-shaped, blooming from a single stalk, a characteristic of the Allium family. Fruits and seeds also play an essential role in plant identification. They are the means by which plants reproduce and spread. The shape, color, and texture of the fruit, the type of seed, and even how it disperses can tell you a lot about the plant.

Putting It All Together: Each of these components of a plant provides a piece of the puzzle in plant identification. It's essential to remember that all these parts work together and interact with each other in different ways depending on the plant species. The key to successful plant identification is looking at the plant as a whole and not just focusing on one single part.

Consider the plant called Lamb's Quarters, a common edible weed. Its leaves are diamond-shaped, and the younger ones often have a whitish powder coating. The flowers are tiny and form a clustered spike at the top of the plant. If you found a plant with similar characteristics, you could tentatively identify it as Lamb's Quarters. But remember, a definitive identification should include checking all the plant's characteristics against a reliable resource, like this book or a plant identification guide.

Identifying plants is a skill, and like any skill, it requires practice. Don't be discouraged if you can't immediately identify every plant you come across. It's a learning process. Take your time to observe, take notes, make sketches, or take pictures. Over time, as you become familiar with more species, you'll start to notice patterns and characteristics that will make identification easier.

As we journey through the world of foraging, always remember to be sure of a plant's identification before you consume it. There are many harmful plants out there that resemble edible ones. But don't let this discourage you. With careful observation, continuous learning, and a healthy dose of respect for nature, you'll be able to unlock the secrets of the plant world and enjoy the wonderful world of foraging.

In the following sections, we'll delve deeper into the profiles of common edible plants and discuss strategies to avoid confusing them with their poisonous lookalikes.

Detailed Profiles of Common Edible Plants

In our journey of understanding the deep-rooted relationship between humans and plants, we now venture into the detailed exploration of common edible plants. This section offers an in-depth analysis of some well-known edible plants, highlighting their unique characteristics, natural habitats, and their various uses in our diets and everyday life. This detailed scrutiny will furnish a diverse palette of knowledge about the edible plants that have played crucial roles in human survival and advancement over centuries.

1. Wheat (Triticum spp.)

Wheat is an indispensable crop, forming the backbone of our diets in many parts of the world. It's a grass widely cultivated for its seed, a cereal grain that is a global staple food.

Description: Wheat plants typically grow to about 2 to 4 feet tall. The plant has hollow stems, slender leaves, and the heads that contain the grains are usually erect and not particularly large. The grains are small, typically a few millimeters long, and range from a pale yellow to a reddish-brown color.

Habitat: Native to the Middle East, wheat has spread across the globe and is now cultivated in countless countries. It is a robust plant that can thrive in a wide range of climates, from the temperate climate zones to subtropical and high altitude tropical regions. Wheat prefers well-drained fertile soil but can adapt to a variety of soil types.

Uses: Beyond bread and pasta, wheat is used to make a wide array of food products, including biscuits, cakes, breakfast cereals, and even alcoholic beverages such as beer and vodka. Wheat is also used as animal feed, and its straw can be used for various purposes like fuel, bedding, or thatching.

2. Rice (Oryza sativa)

Rice is the most important staple food for a large part of the world's human population, especially in Asia, where it is central to several cultures.

Description: Rice plants are typically about 2 to 6 feet high, with a narrow, upright leaf blade and a tassel-like inflorescence at the top where the grains form. The grains are usually white or brown, depending on whether they have been hulled or not.

Habitat: Native to tropical and subtropical southern Asia and Africa, rice is grown in flooded conditions, called paddy fields. It thrives best in regions with high humidity and temperatures consistently above 20 degrees Celsius.

Uses: In addition to being a fundamental part of many cuisines, rice is also used to make flour, syrups, and beverages such as sake. Rice bran can be used to produce oil. The straw is used as animal feed, bedding, and for thatching roofs.

3. Corn (Zea mays)

Corn, or maize, is another principal staple food grown extensively in many parts of the world, especially in the Americas where it originates.

Description: Corn plants can reach heights of 7 to 10 feet and are easily recognized by their tassel-topped stalks and large, broad leaves. The grains, or kernels, form on a cob and are protected by a leafy husk. Kernels can be white, yellow, red, or even purple and black.

Habitat: Corn prefers warm, frost-free weather and is most commonly grown in regions with long, warm summers. It is a versatile plant that can be grown in various types of soil, provided it is well-drained and rich in organic matter.

Uses: Corn is a versatile crop used in numerous dishes, from tortillas and tamales in Mexican cuisine to polenta in Italian cuisine. It's also used in the production of cornstarch, corn syrup, and biofuel. Corn is a significant source of livestock feed as well.

4. Potatoes (Solanum tuberosum)

Potatoes are starchy tubers and are the world's fourth-largest food crop, following rice, wheat, and corn.

Description: The potato plant is a herbaceous perennial that grows about 2 feet tall, notable for its compound leaves and white or lavender flowers. The edible part of the plant is the tuber that grows beneath the soil surface.

Habitat: Originally from the Andean region in South America, potatoes are adaptable and can be grown in a wide range of climates and soils, although they prefer cool weather and well-drained, loamy soil.

Uses: Potatoes are incredibly versatile in culinary applications. They can be baked, boiled, roasted, mashed, or fried. They are used to make chips, crisps, and are also a key ingredient in many dishes, from the British jacket potato to the Indian aloo gobi.

5. Dandelion (Taraxacum officinale)

Often overlooked and dismissed as a simple weed, dandelions are a powerhouse of nutrition that can be found in many temperate regions worldwide.

Description: Dandelions are perennial plants with deeply toothed, lance-shaped leaves, growing in a rosette pattern. They are known for their yellow composite flowers and iconic spherical seed heads, which are dispersed by wind.

Habitat: Originally native to Europe and Asia, dandelions are now widespread in temperate regions around the world. They thrive in a broad range of conditions but are most often found in sunny and well-drained areas.

Uses: Almost all parts of the dandelion are edible. The leaves can be used in salads or sautéed as a side dish. Dandelion flowers can be made into wine, while the roots can be dried, roasted, and ground as a caffeine-free coffee substitute. It's also used medicinally, often as a diuretic.

6. Nettles (Urtica dioica)

Nettles, often avoided due to their stinging hairs, are packed full of nutrients and have a long history of use as a culinary and medicinal herb.

Description: Nettles are perennial herbs with heart-shaped leaves and tiny greenish-white flowers. The whole plant, particularly the leaves, is covered with tiny stinging hairs.

Habitat: Nettles are native to Europe, Asia, northern Africa, and North America, and they thrive in rich soil in partial shade. They're often found growing in woodlands, hedgerows, and near water sources.

Uses: The young leaves, when cooked, lose their sting and can be eaten like spinach. They're a rich source of iron, vitamins, and proteins. Nettles can also be used to make herbal tea and soup. In the textile industry, the fibrous stems of nettles have been used as a cloth material.

7. Purslane (Portulaca oleracea)

Often found in the cracks of a sidewalk or the corners of gardens, Purslane is an often-overlooked edible weed that is common in many parts of the world.

Description: Purslane is a succulent plant with a sprawling growth habit. It has thick, reddish stems and fleshy green leaves, and yellow flowers that only open for a few hours each day.

Habitat: Purslane is highly adaptable and is found in many parts of the world, thriving in a variety of climates. It prefers sandy, well-drained soil, and is often found in gardens and fields, and along roadsides.

Uses: Purslane leaves and stems are edible raw or cooked. They have a slightly sour taste and can be added to salads, stir-fried, or used in soups and stews. The plant is rich in Omega-3 fatty acids and antioxidants.

8. Chickweed (Stellaria media)

Chickweed, a common plant found in many parts of the world, is another edible plant that is often disregarded as a weed.

Description: Chickweed is a cool-season annual plant with small, star-shaped white flowers. It has oval leaves arranged opposite along the stem and grows in a unique, sprawling, mat-like pattern.

Habitat: Chickweed is native to Europe but has spread worldwide. It is a common weed in gardens and fields and prefers fertile, well-drained soil.

Uses: Chickweed can be eaten raw or cooked. Its mild flavor makes it an excellent addition to salads or as a green vegetable. It can also be used in soups and stews. The plant is known for its high vitamin C and mineral content.

These less-known but widely available edible plants offer us a glimpse into the diversity of our natural environment. Recognizing their value not only enriches our diets but also helps us develop a more sustainable and resilient relationship with our food systems.

Dangerous Lookalikes

The art of foraging is a delicate dance with nature, requiring not only an understanding of edible plants but a keen eye for identifying their hazardous lookalikes. In this section, we delve deeper into the world of poisonous plants, outlining their critical identifiers and distinguishing features to help you steer clear of these dangerous botanical doppelgängers. The emphasis lies in ensuring safety by understanding the subtleties and complexities of the plant kingdom.

Our first pair of similar-looking plants are the wild carrot (Daucus carota), a safe and nutritious plant, and the lethal poison hemlock (Conium maculatum). Wild carrot, also known as Queen Anne's Lace, sports delicate clusters of small white flowers, usually featuring a solitary dark purple flower in the center. The finely divided, fern-like leaves are another identifying characteristic. Crushing the roots releases a distinct carrot-like aroma, another key identifier. Its stems are slightly hairy, distinguishing it from its dangerous lookalike.

The poison hemlock, in contrast, is a taller plant with hollow, hairless stems marked with purple blotches – a significant identifier. Its leaves, too, are finely divided but are glossier and emit a somewhat musty odor when crushed. Hemlock's flowers also cluster into umbrella-like shapes but lack the characteristic central purple flower of the wild carrot. Although these differences may seem subtle, they're vital in avoiding potential fatality.

The next duo is the much-coveted morel mushrooms (Morchella genus) and their toxic imitators, the false morels (Gyromitra genus). True morels are a delight for any forager – easily identified by their unique honeycomb cap, they're delicious and safe to eat. However, false morels, sporting a brain-like or wrinkled cap, can often lead to severe poisoning.

Here, it's the interior of the cap that acts as a crucial differentiator. True morels are entirely hollow from the base to the cap – a consistent feature across all stages and sizes. Conversely, false morels will often have a cottony or chambered interior. This feature, along with the brain-like wrinkles rather than honeycomb patterns, can help avoid mistaking false morels for their edible counterparts.

Next, we compare the edible wild garlic (Allium ursinum) and the poisonous lily of the valley (Convallaria majalis). Both these plants sport broad, oval leaves and are often found growing in the same shady woodland habitats. However, a simple crush test can save one from misidentifying these plants. When crushed, wild garlic leaves release a strong garlic aroma, a feature absent in the lily of the valley. Moreover, while wild garlic flowers in clusters of star-like white flowers, lily of the valley bears tiny, bell-shaped flowers along the stem.

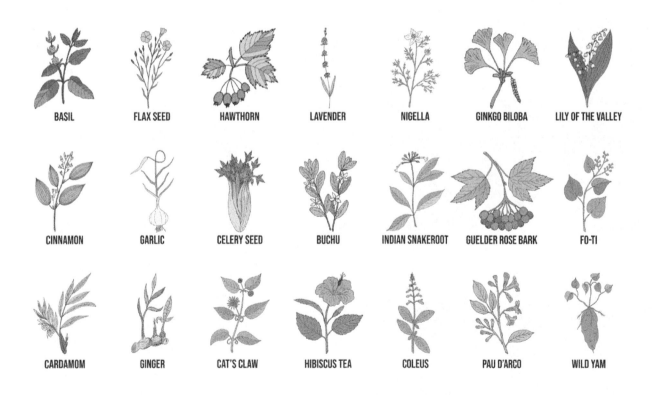

BASIL   FLAX SEED   HAWTHORN   LAVENDER   NIGELLA   GINKGO BILOBA   LILY OF THE VALLEY

CINNAMON   GARLIC   CELERY SEED   BUCHU   INDIAN SNAKEROOT   GUELDER ROSE BARK   FO-TI

CARDAMOM   GINGER   CAT'S CLAW   HIBISCUS TEA   COLEUS   PAU D'ARCO   WILD YAM

Furthermore, there's a pair of berry-bearing plants that often lead to misidentification – the nutritious elderberry (Sambucus nigra) and the deadly poisonous daphne (Daphne mezereum). Both plants bear clusters of bright purple to black berries, but elderberries hang in heavy, drooping clusters, while daphne berries are held erect on the branches. Additionally, elderberry's compound leaves, comprised of five to nine leaflets, differ from daphne's simple, non-divided leaves.

Among the deadliest lookalikes are the death cap (Amanita phalloides) and the destroying angel (Amanita virosa) mushrooms. These fungi can be easily misidentified due to their resemblance to several edible species. For instance, the death cap can be mistaken for the paddy straw mushroom, popular in Asian cuisine, while the destroying angel closely resembles the edible button mushroom.

Amanita phalloides:

Amanita Virosa:

The death cap typically has a greenish, yellowish cap, and white gills that don't attach to the stem. It has a distinct cup or sac at the base of the stem – a telltale sign of poisonous Amanita mushrooms. The destroying angel, in contrast, is entirely white, including its gills, stem, and cap. It also possesses the cup-like sac at the stem's base. Despite the temptation, it's best to avoid any wild white-capped mushroom, considering the high risks involved.

While these descriptions provide detailed differentiation between dangerous and safe plants, they are not exhaustive. Many factors, such as a plant's lifecycle stage, the season, and the specific environment it's growing in, can influence its appearance. It is crucial to cross-reference with reliable field guides and, ideally, consult with local foraging experts or botanists.

This deeper exploration into the world of poisonous plants and their edible lookalikes is a stark reminder that informed foraging is not just about knowing what's safe to eat. It is equally about recognizing what's not. Such knowledge not only ensures our safety but also preserves the respect and harmony we share with nature. Remember, the goal is not just to survive but to thrive while respecting our surrounding ecosystems. This mindfulness ensures the sustainable continuity of foraging traditions for future generations.

With continuous learning, patience, and practical field experience, we can safely navigate the intricate world of wild edibles. Each foraging trip is an opportunity to expand our knowledge, sharpen our observational skills, and deepen our connection with nature. As we foster this relationship with the natural world, we ensure our safety and enrich our foraging experiences.

Chapter 4
Harvesting Techniques

Navigating the wild world of foraging involves more than just knowing what to look for and where. Once you've identified the edible plants in your vicinity and have checked twice, thrice, or even more times for any dangerous lookalikes, the next step in the process is just as important: the act of harvesting.

Harvesting, in the context of foraging, is the careful and sustainable collection of plant materials for consumption. It's not as simple as grabbing a handful of leaves or berries and tossing them into your basket. The act requires finesse, knowledge, respect, and an understanding of the ecological implications of your actions.

This chapter delves into the art of harvesting, focusing on various techniques suitable for different kinds of plants and situations. These range from the correct way to pluck leaves to how to gently uproot a whole plant without causing unnecessary damage to the surroundings. Our goal is to equip you with the skills needed to be an effective and responsible forager.

We will also discuss the importance of timing your harvest to coincide with the plant's life cycle, ensuring you gather them at their nutritional peak. Just as crucial is the process of properly storing and preserving your finds, to keep them at their freshest until they're ready to be used.

By the end of this chapter, you'll have a robust understanding of how to carefully and respectfully gather what nature has to offer. Armed with this knowledge, you can ensure the continuity of foraging traditions, promoting the sustainable use of natural resources.

Timing is Everything: When to Harvest for Optimal Quality

A critical factor that directly influences the quality of foraged edibles is timing. Picking plants at the right time ensures that they are at their nutritional peak, providing the best possible flavors and health benefits. Like the art of foraging itself, the skill of discerning when to harvest different plant species necessitates knowledge, experience, and a fair share of patience.

Many factors contribute to the optimal harvesting time for each plant species, including their life cycle stages, seasonal changes, local climate, and daily weather patterns. Plants, like all organisms, experience different phases of growth and development throughout their life cycles. Each stage corresponds to different chemical compositions within the plant, which, in turn, affect their taste, texture, and nutritional value.

For instance, early spring is typically the best time to harvest young shoots, leaves, and buds when they're tender and sweet. As plants mature through the spring and summer, they divert their energy towards flowering and fruit production. Therefore, summer and early fall often represent the perfect moment to collect fruits, berries, and seeds, which are ripe and abundant. Late fall and winter, while seemingly barren, are prime times for harvesting roots and barks when the plant's energy reserves are concentrated below ground.

However, understanding these general patterns is only the starting point. Each plant species has its unique life cycle and responds differently to seasonal changes. For example, ramps (wild leeks) are one of the first plants to appear in the spring. They must be harvested before their leaves fully unfurl and become tough and bitter. On the other hand, rose hips, the fruit of wild roses, are best harvested after the first frost in the fall, which helps to sweeten them.

Similarly, timing can also be influenced by daily weather patterns. A classic example is wild mushrooms, some species of which are more likely to appear after heavy rains. Conversely, many leafy plants are best harvested early in the morning, when their water content is highest, before the heat of the day causes them to wilt and lose vitality.

A conscientious forager understands that harvesting at the right time is not just about achieving the best taste and nutrition. It is also an essential part of sustainable foraging practices. Harvesting non-renewable parts of a plant, such as its roots or entire body, should be done at the end of its life cycle, allowing it to complete its reproductive process. Furthermore, some plants, like the American Ginseng, should only be harvested during specific legal seasons to prevent overharvesting.

While this might sound overwhelming, especially to the novice forager, fear not. With time and continued practice, recognizing the ideal harvesting time for different species will become second nature. You will learn to read the signs in the landscape, in the plant's appearance, and even in the shifting quality of the air.

The goal here is not to rush the process but to develop a deep relationship with nature. A true forager is a part-time botanist, a part-time ecologist, and a part-time chef. The forager recognizes the intricate web of life that intertwines each plant species with its surrounding ecosystem, including humans. And it is this deep understanding and appreciation that make the practice of foraging not just a way to procure food, but also a way to reconnect with nature on a profound level.

As we journey through this chapter, we will examine specific examples of plants commonly found in North America, understanding their unique harvesting times and the reasons behind them. In doing so, we will shed light on the fascinating world of plants, revealing the intricate dance of life that unfolds across the seasons. In learning how to partake in this dance responsibly, we are taking a significant step towards becoming not just foragers, but stewards of our natural environment.

Harvesting Techniques: How to Harvest Without Harming the Plant

Becoming a responsible and ethical forager involves developing a strong understanding of the plants you're harvesting, their growth patterns, and how to collect them in a way that promotes their continued proliferation. Each plant requires its own unique method of harvesting, depending on which parts are being collected. Let's discuss specific techniques for common types of plants and their respective parts.

1. Harvesting Leaves and Shoots

Consider, for example, a wild dandelion, Taraxacum officinale. When harvesting its leaves for a salad or as a spinach substitute, use a clean, sharp tool like scissors or a knife. Do not yank the leaves, as this can damage the plant. Instead, cut the leaf at the stem junction, leaving the core of the plant intact for future growth. The same rule applies to many other leafy greens, such as wild sorrel or watercress.

If we move to the case of asparagus (Asparagus officinalis), you're after the shoots. Harvest these by snapping them off at the base when they are no more than 8 inches tall. The remaining plant will continue to mature and reproduce, ensuring future crops.

2. Harvesting Flowers and Seeds

Let's consider the case of elderberries (Sambucus). When collecting their flowers to make a refreshing elderflower cordial, ensure you cut the whole flower head, not individual flowers. The plant will continue its growth cycle and move on to produce fruits, ensuring seeds for future seasons.

When it comes to harvesting seeds, take the example of wild sunflowers (Helianthus). Wait until the flower heads are brown and the back of the head is yellow, then cut it off with about a foot of stem. Hang it upside down to fully dry before shaking out the seeds.

3. Harvesting Fruits and Berries

Fruits and berries require a delicate touch. For example, when harvesting wild blackberries (Rubus fruticosus), gently pull the ripe fruit. If it doesn't detach easily, it isn't ripe yet. Avoid yanking or pulling hard to prevent damaging the plant or its unripe fruits.

The same gentleness applies to wild apples (Malus domestica). Twist the fruit gently; if it's ripe, it will come away easily. Avoid shaking the tree or breaking branches, which can harm the tree and reduce future harvests.

4. Harvesting Roots and Barks

Root harvesting is often the most invasive and potentially harmful. Wild ginseng (Panax quinquefolius) is a great example. After identifying a mature plant (usually 5-10 years old), dig carefully around the root with a narrow trowel, taking care not to damage it. Harvest only a portion of the root, then replace the soil and leaf litter to help the remaining plant parts regrow.

When harvesting bark, such as from the white willow (Salix alba) for its salicylic acid, make a single, vertical cut in the tree's bark and peel off a small strip. Never remove bark all the way around the tree – a practice called "ring-barking" – as it cuts off the tree's nutrient supply and will kill it.

5. General Techniques and Ethics

Irrespective of the plant or the part being harvested, always use clean, sharp tools to prevent plant infections. Respect private property and protected areas, seek permission where required, and adhere to all foraging laws.

Ensure you follow a "leave no trace" approach to foraging. Take only what you need and leave the environment as you found it, or better. Sustainable foraging is not just about the harvest; it's about building a relationship with nature and contributing to the preservation of our ecosystems.

Unique Harvesting Techniques

Certain plants necessitate special consideration when it comes to harvesting due to their unique growth habits, fragility, or the specific plant parts being collected. In this section, we'll explore several examples of such plants and discuss the best practices for harvesting them.

1. Harvesting Nettles (Urtica dioica)
One of the first plants that necessitates a unique harvesting technique is the stinging nettle. Nettles, which are known for their painful sting if touched, are a nutritional powerhouse, packed with vitamins, minerals, and even protein. To harvest them safely, you'll need a pair of gloves and a good pair of scissors. When picking, always cut above a node or a pair of leaves to encourage regrowth. Snip off the top few inches of the plant, which will be the most tender and flavorful part.

2. Harvesting Cattails (Typha)

Cattails are a highly versatile plant, with every part of the plant having a use at different times of the year. When collecting the young shoots in spring, they can be snapped off close to the base. But be careful not to pull the whole plant out from the water or marsh in which it's growing. Later in the year, the yellow pollen can be harvested by shaking the flowering head into a bag. To collect the rootstocks for their starch content, carefully dig around the base of the plant, trying not to disrupt neighboring plants.

3. Harvesting Fiddleheads (Matteuccia struthiopteris)

Fiddleheads, the curled fronds of young ostrich ferns, are a spring delicacy, but they must be harvested judiciously to protect the long-term health of the fern colony. A general rule is to harvest no more than half the fiddleheads from each crown and to only collect from colonies with six or more crowns. By leaving enough fiddleheads to mature into ferns, the colony can photosynthesize, store energy, and thrive for years to come.

4. Harvesting Ramps or Wild Leeks (Allium tricoccum)

Ramps have become extremely popular, and overharvesting is now a significant problem. If you find a patch, consider harvesting only the leaves, which are flavorful and leave the bulbs to grow for next year. If you do want to collect the bulbs, take no more than 10% from any patch and carefully replace the soil and leaf litter afterward.

5. Harvesting Morel Mushrooms (Morchella)

While not a plant, morel mushrooms require unique considerations. Morels are mycorrhizal, meaning they form a symbiotic relationship with trees. The mushrooms you see are the fruiting bodies of a larger organism that lives under the soil. Overharvesting can harm these delicate subterranean networks. When harvesting morels, it's best to cut the mushroom at the base with a knife, leaving the root-like structure (mycelium) in the ground. Carry your harvest in a mesh bag to allow spores to spread as you continue your foraging.

6. Harvesting Prickly Pear Cactus (Opuntia)

In drier areas, the prickly pear cactus can provide a bounty of edible pads and fruits, but they require careful handling due to their spines. It's best to use tongs or a forked stick to twist the fruits or pads from the cactus. Then, using a stick or knife, remove the spines before handling them further.

7. Harvesting Pine Nuts (Pinus edulis and others)

Harvesting pine nuts involves collecting the cones from certain pine species. This can be a tricky endeavor as the cones need to be harvested when they're mature but before they fully open. This usually means reaching high into the trees with a long pole or climbing. Once on the ground, the cones should be stored in a warm, dry place and allowed to dry out and open naturally. The seeds can then be shaken out or removed with tweezers.

These are just a few examples of how different plants require unique harvesting techniques. As you grow in your foraging journey, you'll develop an ever-deepening understanding of the plants around you, and how best to harvest them in a way that supports their continued growth and vitality.

We have journeyed through the world of harvesting techniques, paying close attention to the intricacies of the timing, approach, and specific considerations for unique plant species. Harvesting isn't just about gathering what you need from nature; it's about respecting each plant's characteristics, knowing its lifecycle, and understanding how to collect in a manner that is sustainable and non-damaging.

We have learned that timing is an essential factor in foraging, as it can significantly impact the quality and nutritional content of the harvested plant parts. A deep understanding of the changing seasons, growth patterns, and lifecycle stages of plants is crucial to ensure optimal harvesting times. This knowledge is as varied as nature itself and requires an attentive eye and a passion for understanding the rhythms of the natural world.

Furthermore, we delved into the various techniques of harvesting, focusing on how to do so without harming the plants or disrupting their natural habitats. We have explored several tools and practices, from simply using your hands to the careful employment of knives, scissors, and other specialized equipment. The most crucial point is to ensure we are not over-harvesting or causing unnecessary damage to the plants or their surrounding environment.

Finally, we looked at several specific plants that require unique considerations during harvesting due to their growth habits, fragility, or the particular parts being collected. From stinging nettles to cattails, fiddleheads to ramps, morels to prickly pear cactuses, and even pine trees, we've seen how each species has its unique requirements and ways to ensure their continued growth and vitality.

I hope that this chapter has provided you with valuable insights into the delicate art of plant harvesting. The knowledge, practices, and skills we've shared are not only about foraging for food or other uses, but they are also a testament to our role as caretakers of the environment.

Chapter 5
Preparing Your Foraged Finds

The world of foraging brings us closer to the ground, both metaphorically and literally. It roots us back to the simplicity of nature and teaches us the values of sustainability, resourcefulness, and respect for the Earth's bounty. However, foraging doesn't stop when we exit the forest or the field, basket filled with natural treasures. The culmination of this beautiful journey lies in what we do after the foraging—how we transform these gifts of nature into something we can consume, use, or share.

Welcome to Chapter 5, "Preparing Your Foraged Finds". This chapter will guide you through the exciting journey of preparing, processing, and using your foraged finds in the most effective and nourishing ways possible. This is where foraging meets the art of cooking and crafting, where the raw ingredients you've painstakingly harvested are turned into delicious meals, healing remedies, or other useful items.

In this chapter, we will cover how to clean and store your foraged goods to maximize their shelf life and nutritional value. We'll explore the various ways of cooking, preserving, and fermenting, the unique and delicious recipes you can create, and how to make and use natural remedies. Each section will provide you with detailed, easy-to-follow steps, tips and tricks, and plenty of practical examples.

However, remember that this chapter is about more than just instruction—it's about fostering a deeper connection between you and the food you consume or the remedies you use. It's about knowing the story behind each ingredient, understanding the effort and respect involved in its collection, and valuing the journey it took from the wilderness to your home. So let's dive in and discover how to honor the fruits of your foraging through mindful preparation and use.

From Field to Table: Cleaning and Preparing Wild Edibles

Once you've stepped off the forest trail and into your kitchen, the harvested treasures in your basket embark on a transformative journey. The wild edibles you've carefully collected now require cleaning, preparing, and, eventually, cooking, turning these nature-born ingredients into nourishing meals. This section, "From Field to Table: Cleaning and Preparing Wild Edibles," will walk you through the crucial steps to transition your foraged finds from raw ingredients to recipe-ready.

Let's start at the very beginning with your arrival back home from a day's foraging. The diverse mix of wild edibles you've collected—whether they're berries, mushrooms, herbs, or roots—requires careful sorting. First, lay out your foraged goods on a clean surface and divide them into categories. This simple act makes the subsequent cleaning and preparing process easier and more effective.

Next, we move onto cleaning. It's a crucial step to ensure the safety and quality of your foraged foods. The main goal here is to remove any unwanted debris, insects, or dirt, while preserving the integrity of the plant material.

For most leafy greens and flowers, a gentle shake before you place them in your foraging basket is often sufficient. However, once home, submerge them in a bowl of cool water, gently swishing them around to dislodge any stubborn grit or tiny insects. Lift the leaves or flowers out of the water rather than draining the whole bowl—this way, any dirt will be left behind in the bowl.

Berries demand a delicate hand. Rinse them under a slow stream of cool water, gently turning them to ensure all sides are cleaned. A soft brush can be used for tough-skinned fruits like wild apples or pears, scrubbing off any surface dirt or tiny insects. For smaller and more delicate berries, consider soaking them in cool water with a dash of vinegar, which helps to kill any bacteria. However, remember to rinse them with fresh water afterward to remove any vinegar taste.

Mushrooms require a unique approach. Traditional advice suggests not to wash mushrooms as they absorb water. However, food safety experts agree that it's perfectly safe to rinse or quickly dunk mushrooms in water to remove any dirt. For more stubborn debris in gilled mushrooms, use a soft brush or a damp paper towel. Always remember to handle mushrooms gently to maintain their structure and flavor.

Roots like wild carrots or burdock can be brushed to remove the soil, rinsed, and then peeled, similar to their domestic counterparts.

After cleaning, we move to the preparation phase, which varies depending on the type of wild edible and the dish you're planning. Leafy greens are often best when they're chopped into salads or added to soups towards the end of the cooking process. Berries can be enjoyed fresh, used in baking, or made into sauces or jams.

Herbs can be minced or used whole, depending on the recipe. For instance, wild garlic can be used similarly to cultivated garlic, minced, and added to a wide range of dishes for a flavorful punch. Wild mint, on the other hand, is excellent in refreshing beverages, or it can be steeped in hot water for a soothing tea.

Roots require more thorough cooking to break down their fibrous content. They can be boiled, baked, or fried. Wild carrots can be used in the same manner as domestic carrots, great in soups or stews, while burdock roots are delightful when thinly sliced and stir-fried.

Mushrooms offer a vast array of preparation methods, from simple sautéing in butter to more complex dishes like stews and risottos. Morels, for instance, are delicious when lightly breaded and pan-fried, while porcini are great in pasta or risotto.

In essence, the journey from field to table is as rewarding as the foraging excursion itself. As you clean and prepare your wild edibles, remember to handle them with care, honoring the life they once held, the hands that harvested them, and the nourishment they will soon provide.

Cooking Wild

Taking the leap from foraging and preparing to actually cooking your wild finds is an exciting step in your journey of wild food exploration. This chapter, will illuminate the various cooking methods you can employ to turn your foraged goods into nutritious, flavorful meals. From the gentle simmer of a pot filled with fragrant herbs to the sizzling sear of mushrooms on a hot pan, there's a plethora of techniques to discover.

We'll begin with an overview of some basic cooking techniques suitable for a variety of wild foods. These include sautéing, roasting, steaming, and slow cooking. While these methods might be familiar from cooking traditional ingredients, the use of wild edibles brings about unique considerations and opportunities for creativity.

Sautéing is a fast, high-heat cooking method that's ideal for many wild foods, particularly mushrooms and leafy greens. Wild garlic, nettles, and dandelion greens can be lightly sautéed in a bit of oil and garlic for a quick and delicious side dish. For example, sauté wild garlic in a splash of olive oil with a sprinkle of sea salt. When they're wilted and lightly golden, finish them with a squeeze of fresh lemon juice for a bright and nutritious side dish.

Roasting, on the other hand, is a slower, lower-heat method that works well for root vegetables like wild carrots, burdock, and Jerusalem artichokes. Toss your roots in olive oil, season with salt and pepper, and roast them in a hot oven until they're tender and caramelized. For an extra layer of flavor, consider adding a sprinkling of wild herbs like rosemary or thyme towards the end of the cooking time.

Steaming is a gentle cooking method that can preserve the delicate flavors and nutrients of wild greens and flowers. Edible flowers like elderflowers or violets can be steamed and then added to salads or used as a garnish for a wild-foraged feast.

Slow cooking is excellent for tougher wild edibles like roots and certain mushrooms. Morels, for instance, can be slowly simmered in a cream sauce to make a decadent pasta topping.

With a grounding in these cooking techniques, let's now explore some specific recipes that showcase the unique flavors and textures of wild foods.

A forager's breakfast might feature Wild Garlic and Nettle Frittata. Start by sautéing chopped wild garlic and nettles in olive oil until they're wilted. Beat some eggs in a bowl, season with salt and pepper, then pour over the greens. Cook gently until the eggs are set, then finish under a broiler until golden and slightly puffed. The result is a hearty, flavorful breakfast that's a beautiful celebration of springtime foraging.

For a light lunch, a Wild Green Salad with a Dandelion Vinaigrette offers a fresh take on a classic dish. Gather a mix of wild greens like dandelion leaves, chickweed, and sorrel, then toss with a dressing made from dandelion flower-infused vinegar, olive oil, honey, and a pinch of salt. This salad is a celebration of the diverse range of flavors found in wild greens, from the slightly bitter dandelion leaves to the tangy sorrel.

At dinner, a Foraged Mushroom Risotto lets the robust flavors of wild mushrooms shine. Sauté a mix of wild mushrooms like chanterelles, porcini, and morels in olive oil and butter, then set aside. In the same pan, sauté chopped onions until translucent, add Arborio rice, and cook until the rice is lightly toasted. Gradually add hot vegetable broth, stirring until each addition is absorbed before adding more. Once the rice is cooked, stir in the mushrooms, a generous handful of grated Parmesan cheese, and a knob of butter. The result is a creamy, flavorful risotto that showcases the unique flavors and textures of wild mushrooms.

Finally, no wild food feast would be complete without dessert. A Wild Berry Galette is a simple yet impressive way to show off the flavors of foraged berries. Make a simple pastry, then fill with a mix of wild berries like blackberries, raspberries, and bilberries. Sprinkle with sugar, fold over the edges of the pastry, and bake until golden and bubbling. The result is a rustic, fruit-forward dessert that's a sweet end to a meal of wild foods.

Wild Quick Cookbook

Wild Garlic and Nettle Frittata

Preparation Time: 20 minutes

Ingredients: 1 cup chopped wild garlic, 1 cup chopped nettles, 6 eggs, 2 tablespoons olive oil, Salt and pepper to taste, Juice of half a lemon

Procedure: Start by sautéing the wild garlic and nettles in the olive oil until wilted. Beat the eggs, add salt and pepper, and pour over the sautéed greens. Cook on low heat until the eggs are set, then finish under the broiler until golden.

Calories: Approximately 300 per serving

Wild Green Salad with Dandelion Vinaigrette

Preparation Time: 15 minutes

Ingredients: 4 cups mixed wild greens (dandelion leaves, chickweed, sorrel), For the vinaigrette - 3 tablespoons dandelion flower-infused vinegar, 6 tablespoons olive oil, 1 teaspoon honey, Salt to taste

Procedure: Toss the wild greens in a large bowl. Whisk together the vinaigrette ingredients until well combined. Drizzle the vinaigrette over the greens and toss until evenly coated.

Calories: Approximately 200 per serving

Foraged Mushroom Risotto

Preparation Time: 1 hour

Ingredients: 1 cup mixed wild mushrooms (chanterelles, porcini, morels), 1 cup Arborio rice, 1 chopped onion, 1 quart vegetable broth, 1/2 cup grated Parmesan cheese, 2 tablespoons butter, 2 tablespoons olive oil

Procedure: Sauté the mushrooms in the olive oil and 1 tablespoon of butter, then set aside. Sauté the onion in the same pan until translucent, add the rice and cook until lightly toasted. Gradually add the hot broth, stirring until each addition is absorbed before adding more. Once the rice is cooked, stir in the mushrooms, Parmesan, and remaining butter.

Calories: Approximately 400 per serving

Roasted Wild Root Vegetables

Preparation Time: 1 hour

Ingredients: 4 cups mixed wild root vegetables (wild carrots, burdock, Jerusalem artichokes), 2 tablespoons olive oil, Salt and pepper to taste, Fresh rosemary or thyme

Procedure: Toss the root vegetables in olive oil, salt, and pepper. Spread them out on a baking sheet and roast at 400 degrees Fahrenheit for about 45 minutes, or until tender and caramelized. Add the fresh herbs in the last 5 minutes of roasting.

Calories: Approximately 200 per serving

Wild Berry Galette

Preparation Time: 1.5 hours

Ingredients: 2 cups mixed wild berries (blackberries, raspberries, bilberries), 1 cup flour, 1/2 cup cold butter, 1/4 cup sugar, 2-3 tablespoons cold water

Procedure: Make the pastry by cutting the butter into the flour until it resembles coarse breadcrumbs. Add the water and knead just until the dough comes together. Roll out the dough and transfer to a baking sheet. Sprinkle the berries and sugar onto the dough, leaving a border around the edge. Fold the edges of the dough over the berries. Bake at 375 degrees Fahrenheit for about 45 minutes, or until the pastry is golden and the berries are bubbling.

Calories: Approximately 300 per serving

The recipes are versatile and can be used at different times of the day based on personal preference. However, here are some suggestions:

1. **Breakfast:**
- Wild Garlic and Nettle Frittata: A protein-packed dish perfect for breakfast or brunch.

2. **Lunch:**
- Wild Green Salad with Dandelion Vinaigrette: This light and refreshing salad is perfect for a midday meal.
- Foraged Mushroom Risotto: Risotto is a satisfying lunch dish, and you can serve it with a side of salad for added balance.

3. **Dinner:**
- Roasted Wild Root Vegetables: These can serve as a side to your main dinner dish, such as grilled meat or fish.
- Foraged Mushroom Risotto: This could also serve as a rich, comforting dinner.

4. **Dessert or Snack:**
- Wild Berry Galette: Perfect for dessert after any meal or as a sweet snack.

Remember that these are just suggestions. The beauty of these dishes is their flexibility. They can be enjoyed at different times of the day based on your dietary needs and preferences.

Nutritional Goldmines

An often-underappreciated aspect of foraged food is the enormous wealth of nutrition they offer. As we dive into this section, we will explore the nutritive richness of these edibles, underscoring the tremendous health benefits they bring.

Wild edibles typically contain a higher concentration of essential nutrients than many cultivated counterparts. The rationale for this can be attributed to the rich and diverse soil conditions in the wild, which allow plants to uptake a variety of minerals. Furthermore, these plants, left to fend for themselves in the wild, have naturally evolved defense mechanisms that result in an array of bioactive compounds beneficial to human health.

For instance, consider dandelions, a plant commonly dismissed as a pesky weed. However, these robust plants are a powerhouse of nutrients. They are rich in Vitamin K, which plays a crucial role in maintaining bone health and assisting in blood coagulation. Dandelions also contain a substantial amount of Vitamin A, important for vision, immune system function, and reproduction. Furthermore, dandelions offer a wealth of minerals like iron, potassium, and calcium.

Stinging nettles are another prime example of a nutritional goldmine. These humble plants offer a plethora of nutrients, including vitamins A, C, and K, along with several B vitamins. They are also packed with minerals such as calcium, iron, magnesium, phosphorus, potassium, and sodium. Stinging nettles also contain a high amount of protein for a plant, which makes them a valuable addition to a plant-based diet. What's more, nettles have been traditionally used for their anti-inflammatory properties and can be a potent ally in fighting seasonal allergies.

Wild garlic, or ramsons, are yet another example of the nutritional wealth offered by wild edibles. It boasts an impressive nutrient profile, including vitamins A and C, calcium, iron, phosphorus, and a whole host of potent plant compounds. It has been suggested that wild garlic can support cardiovascular health due to its high content of allicin, a compound known for its heart-protective properties.

Even fungi, like the popularly foraged Morel mushroom, have their share of nutritional benefits. Morels are rich in Vitamin D, a nutrient that many people lack, especially in the winter months. They are also a good source of iron and have significant amounts of protein.

Let's now turn our attention to the wild berries, specifically the lesser-known elderberries. These dark purple berries are known for their immune-boosting properties, thanks in part to their high Vitamin C content. They also contain a significant amount of dietary fiber, which aids in digestion, and are a source of Vitamin A and several B vitamins.

However, it's crucial to remember that the nutritional content of wild foods can be influenced by various factors. These include the condition of the soil where the plant grew, the time of year the plant was harvested, and the plant's stage of growth at harvest.

While the nutritional profile of these wild edibles is impressive, it's essential to incorporate them into a balanced diet. No single food can provide all the nutrients your body needs. Also, certain wild edibles should be consumed in moderation due to their potent nature.

In summary, the world of wild edibles is a vast nutritional goldmine waiting to be discovered. Incorporating these plants into your diet can significantly enrich your nutrient intake and contribute to a healthier lifestyle. However, caution should be exercised when foraging, and it's important to accurately identify plants to avoid potentially harmful species. By approaching this practice with respect, knowledge, and caution, you can reap the rich bounty that nature has to offer.

With this comprehensive understanding of the nutritional value of wild edibles, we can now appreciate the profound impact that foraging can have on our health, offering not only a way to reconnect with nature but also a means to enhance our wellbeing in a wholesome, natural way.

Rosehip:

Chapter 6
Preserving and Storing Wild Edibles

As we journey deeper into the art of foraging, we move from identifying, harvesting, and cooking wild foods to an equally important aspect of the foraging journey—preserving and storing wild edibles. This chapter, "Preserving and Storing Wild Edibles," takes you through the techniques and strategies needed to extend the life of your wild harvest, ensuring that you can enjoy the bounty of nature's pantry long after the foraging season has ended.

Foraging, in essence, is a cyclical journey. The skills we acquire and the knowledge we gain are deeply tied to the rhythms of nature. When nature is generous, the abundance it offers often surpasses what we can consume at once. As such, understanding the art of preserving and storing wild edibles becomes an integral part of sustainable foraging.

In this chapter, we will explore various traditional and modern preservation techniques, from canning, pickling, and fermenting to drying and freezing. We will learn about the importance of proper storage conditions to maintain the freshness, flavor, and nutritional value of our wild edibles, and we will also discuss the specifics of storing different types of wild foods.

Moreover, we will delve into the intricacies of each preservation method, learning about their advantages, disadvantages, and ideal use-cases. Our aim is to provide you with a comprehensive toolbox that will help you choose the best preservation and storage methods for your foraged goods.

As we delve into this exciting chapter, you will gain valuable insights and practical knowledge that will take your foraging practice to a new level, enabling you to enjoy the fruits of your foraging labor all year round. Let's embark on this exciting journey together and discover how we can make the most of nature's bountiful harvest!

Longevity: Drying and Dehydrating Techniques for Preservation"

Drying and dehydrating are age-old techniques that have been used by civilizations across the world to extend the longevity of their food resources, especially in times of plenty. In this section titled "Longevity: Drying and Dehydrating Techniques for Preservation," we'll journey through these methods to understand how they can be employed effectively in the context of wild edibles.

Let's start with practical examples:

1. Air Drying:

Air drying is perhaps the simplest and most cost-effective method of drying wild edibles, particularly suitable for herbs like rosemary, thyme, and sage. It relies on the circulation of air in a warm, dry environment.

For example, to air-dry foraged dandelion leaves, you would first rinse them thoroughly to remove any dirt or insects. Shake off the excess water and pat the leaves dry using a clean towel. Bundle the stems together and hang them upside down in a warm, well-ventilated area away from direct sunlight. After about two weeks, the leaves should be thoroughly dry and can be stripped from the stems and stored in airtight containers.

2. Oven Drying:

Oven drying is a faster method, ideal for fruits and mushrooms with higher water content.

For instance, let's consider wild apples. After harvesting, wash the apples and slice them thinly, removing any seeds. Arrange the apple slices on a baking sheet lined with parchment paper, ensuring that the slices do not overlap. Set your oven to its lowest temperature setting, usually between 50-70°C (120-160°F), and place the baking sheet inside. Leave the oven door slightly ajar to allow moisture to escape. Depending on the thickness of your slices, it might take several hours for the apples to dry completely.

3. Dehydrator Drying:

A dehydrator provides the most controlled environment for drying, and is excellent for fruits, vegetables, and mushrooms.

Consider dehydrating morels, a popular foraged mushroom. After cleaning the morels, slice them in half lengthwise and arrange them on the dehydrator trays. Set your dehydrator to around 55-60°C (130-140°F). It will typically take 8-10 hours for the morels to dehydrate, but timing may vary depending on the size of the mushrooms and the specific model of your dehydrator.

4. Sun Drying:

Sun drying, as the name suggests, uses the heat of the sun to dry foods. This method is best suited for hot, dry climates and works well for fruits like wild berries. For example, to sun dry blackberries, start by washing and drying the berries. Place them on a tray covered with a clean kitchen towel or cheesecloth. Position the tray in a sunny, well-ventilated location. To protect the berries from insects, you can cover the tray with a mesh screen. It can take several days for the berries to dry fully. Make sure to bring them inside during the night to prevent dew from adding moisture back into the berries.

The essence of drying and dehydrating is moisture removal. By eliminating the water content in the food, we can inhibit the growth of bacteria, yeasts, and molds that cause food spoilage. The result is a shelf-stable product that can be enjoyed far beyond its fresh lifespan, preserving not just the food itself but also a significant portion of its nutritional content.

When it comes to drying and dehydrating wild edibles, the methods employed can vary from simple air drying to more complex processes using dehydrators, ovens, and even smokers. Each method has its specific applications and advantages depending on the type of wild edible being preserved.

Consider, for example, wild mushrooms like the Boletus edulis (Porcini). These mushrooms are a forager's delight, known for their distinct flavor and meaty texture. However, fresh Porcini mushrooms have a short shelf life. By slicing and dehydrating them, we can preserve these wonderful foraged finds for up to a year, enhancing their flavor in the process. The dehydrated Porcini can be rehydrated and used in various dishes, from risottos to stews, all year round.

Similar principles apply to foraged herbs like mint, dandelion, and nettle. Air drying is a straightforward and energy-efficient way to preserve these herbs. After harvesting, the herbs can be bundled and hung upside down in a warm, well-ventilated room away from direct sunlight. In a few weeks, the dried herbs can be stripped from their stems and stored in airtight containers for future use.

Foraging fruits and berries like blackberries, elderberries, and apples can also benefit from dehydration. Drying these fruits intensifies their flavors and makes for a convenient and healthy snack. For best results, slice the fruits uniformly and arrange them in a single layer on the dehydrator trays. The temperature and duration of drying will depend on the specific type of fruit and the dehydrator model.

Yet, it's essential to keep in mind that not all wild edibles are suited for drying or dehydrating. Some wild edibles, particularly those with high water content, may lose their texture and taste when dried. Others may have components that are only activated or destroyed through other forms of preservation or preparation. As such, it's important to research each wild edible you forage before deciding on the best preservation method.

In addition, quality and safety should never be compromised when drying and dehydrating wild edibles. Ensure that the foraged finds are clean, healthy, and free from infestations. Overly mature or damaged specimens may not dry properly and can lead to spoilage.

Understanding and mastering drying and dehydrating techniques open up a new avenue for extending the shelf life of your foraged finds. It allows for the enjoyment of wild edibles well beyond their harvesting season, adding a touch of wilderness to your meals throughout the year. However, it's important to remember that these are not the only preservation techniques at our disposal. In the subsequent sections, we will explore more ways to preserve and store wild edibles, each with its unique benefits and applications.

The Art of Canning

In the realm of food preservation, the technique of canning stands tall as a timeless and effective method. It offers a beautiful way of capturing the freshness and flavors of your foraged finds and preserving them for later use. Alongside canning, the art of pickling too allows you to extend the life of your wild harvests while adding a tangy flavor and a delightful crunch. This section is dedicated to elucidating these preserving techniques with practical examples, allowing you to enjoy the fruits (and vegetables, herbs, and mushrooms) of your foraging labor for months, even years to come.

Canning

Canning involves processing food in closed glass jars to destroy microorganisms and inactivate enzymes that could lead to spoilage. It's a method that's been used for centuries to preserve a wide variety of foods, from fruits and vegetables to meats and seafood. Let's delve into the steps and techniques involved in canning, using the example of wild blackberries.

1.   **Cleaning and Preparation:** Begin by washing your blackberries thoroughly and patting them dry. Any damaged or overripe fruits should be discarded. In the meantime, you can wash your jars, lids, and bands in warm, soapy water.

2.	**Cooking:** Place the blackberries in a large pot and crush them lightly to release their juices. Add sugar according to your preference, then cook over medium heat until the berries are soft and the mixture thickens slightly.

3.	**Filling the Jars:** While the berries are cooking, you can sterilize your jars by boiling them in a large pot of water. Once sterilized, fill the hot jars with the blackberry mixture, leaving a bit of headspace to allow for expansion during processing.

4.	**Sealing and Processing:** After filling the jars, wipe the rims clean, place the lids on top, and screw on the bands until they're fingertip-tight. Submerge the jars in boiling water and process them for the recommended time. For blackberries, that's usually about 10 minutes.

5.	**Cooling and Storage:** Once processed, remove the jars from the water bath and let them cool. As they cool, you should hear a popping sound, indicating a successful seal. After 24 hours, check the seals, then store the jars in a cool, dark place. Your blackberries are now preserved, ready for you to enjoy their summer-fresh taste even in the depths of winter.

Pickling

While canning can preserve a wide range of wild edibles, pickling is a process that takes preservation a step further. By immersing food in a solution of vinegar, salt, and sometimes sugar, you not only preserve your wild harvest but also impart a delightful tangy flavor. To illustrate, let's look at how to pickle wild ramps, a springtime delicacy that's often foraged for its unique garlicky flavor.

1.	**Preparation:** Start by cleaning your ramps. Trim the roots and remove any wilted leaves. Prepare your pickling solution by combining vinegar, water, sugar, and salt in a saucepan and bringing it to a boil.

2.	**Packing and Pouring the Brine:** Pack the cleaned ramps into sterilized jars, fitting as many as you can without crushing them. Pour the hot pickling solution over the ramps, making sure they're fully submerged.

3.   **Sealing and Processing:** Wipe the rims of the jars, place the lids on, and tighten the bands. Process the jars in a boiling water bath for 10 minutes, then remove and allow them to cool.

4.   **Storage:** After the jars have cooled, check the seals. If sealed properly, the pickled ramps can be stored in a cool, dark place for up to a year.

Both canning and pickling can seem a little daunting if you're new to it, but with some practice, you'll find that they're straightforward and enjoyable ways to extend the shelf life of your foraged foods. The key to successful preservation lies in maintaining cleanliness and following proper processing times. With these skills in hand, you can enjoy the fruits of your foraging expeditions long after the season has passed.

Cold Storage

When it comes to preserving our wild edibles, freezing is undeniably one of the most convenient and effective methods available to us. It requires little to no pre-treatment and often allows the food to retain more of its nutritional value than other preservation methods. However, not all wild edibles are suitable for freezing. Thus, understanding the appropriate techniques and considerations can help you make the best use of this method.

In this section, we will explore the freezing technique for five different categories of wild edibles: fruits, vegetables, mushrooms, herbs, and nuts, each of which requires a slightly different approach. With each example, we'll explore the unique considerations and steps that go into freezing these wild foods, helping you to maintain their quality, nutrition, and flavor.

Fruits: Freezing Wild Blackberries

1. **Cleaning and Preparation:** Start by washing the blackberries gently under cool running water and letting them dry completely. This can be facilitated by laying them out on a kitchen towel and patting them gently.

2. **Pre-Freezing:** To prevent the fruits from clumping together during freezing, spread the berries out on a baking sheet lined with parchment paper and put them in the freezer. This is often referred to as 'flash freezing.'

3. **Packing:** Once the berries are frozen solid, transfer them into airtight freezer bags. Squeeze out as much air as possible before sealing the bags to prevent freezer burn.

4. **Storage:** Label the bags with the date and contents, then store them in the freezer. Frozen blackberries can be used directly from the freezer in smoothies, baked goods, and sauces.

Vegetables: Freezing Fiddlehead Ferns

1. **Cleaning and Blanching:** Clean the fiddleheads thoroughly, removing any brown scales. Then blanch them in boiling water for two minutes. Blanching is a critical step for vegetables, as it halts enzyme activity that could lead to loss of flavor, color, and nutrients.

2. **Cooling and Draining:** After blanching, cool the fiddleheads quickly in ice water to stop the cooking process. Drain them well.

3. **Packing and Storage:** Pack the fiddleheads into freezer bags, remove as much air as possible, then seal, label, and store in the freezer.

Mushrooms: Freezing Morels

1. **Cleaning and Slicing:** Gently clean morels with a soft brush and slice them in half lengthwise. Unlike most vegetables, mushrooms don't need to be blanched before freezing, as the texture change due to enzyme activity isn't as noticeable.

2. **Pre-Freezing and Packing:** Spread the morel halves on a baking sheet and flash freeze them. Once frozen, transfer them to freezer bags, remove as much air as possible, then seal and label.

3. **Storage:** Morels can be stored in the freezer and used directly from frozen in soups, sauces, and other cooked dishes.

Herbs: Freezing Wild Garlic

1. **Cleaning and Chopping:** Clean the wild garlic leaves and pat them dry. Chop the leaves finely.

2. **Packing and Freezing:** Pack the chopped leaves into ice cube trays, filling each cube about two-thirds full. Top up with water, then freeze.

3. **Storage:** Once the cubes are frozen, pop them out of the trays and store them in freezer bags. They can be thrown directly into soups, stews, and stir-fries for a burst of garlic flavor.

Nuts: Freezing Black Walnuts

1.   **Cleaning and Drying:** Remove the husks from the black walnuts and wash the nuts. Let them dry completely.

2.   **Packing and Storage:** Pack the dried nuts into freezer bags, remove as much air as possible, then seal, label, and store in the freezer.

From fruits and vegetables to herbs and nuts, freezing offers an efficient and practical way of preserving a wide range of wild edibles. Each category of food requires a slightly different approach, but by following these guidelines, you can enjoy the fresh flavors and nutrition of your wild harvests throughout the year. As with all preservation methods, the key to successful freezing lies in using high-quality, fresh-picked foods and proper packing and storage techniques.

The value of foraging and harvesting wild edibles lies not just in the gathering process but also in our ability to preserve these natural resources for extended use. In this chapter, we've discussed various techniques for preserving wild edibles, emphasizing drying and dehydrating, canning and pickling, and freezing as three of the most accessible and effective methods.

Each of these methods offers unique benefits and challenges. Drying and dehydrating is an ancient method of preservation that is perfect for long-term storage and requires minimal equipment. Canning and pickling are transformative processes that can add new flavors and textures to your foraged foods, while also offering long shelf life. Freezing, on the other hand, helps retain much of the original texture and nutritional value of your wild edibles and offers the added convenience of easy storage and use.

For each of these preservation methods, we've detailed specific procedures for different categories of wild edibles, from fruits and vegetables to herbs and nuts. We've provided practical examples and tips that you can apply when you embark on your foraging journey.

However, the learning doesn't end here. Just like foraging, preserving wild edibles is as much art as it is science. Experience is a great teacher. As you practice these techniques, you'll come to learn the nuances of each method, which will help you make the most of your wild harvests.

Remember, successful preservation starts with careful harvesting. Choosing high-quality, ripe edibles and handling them gently will ensure the best results, regardless of the preservation method you choose. Also, it's crucial to store your preserved foods properly and monitor them regularly for any signs of spoilage.

Chapter 7
Advanced Foraging Topics

As we journey further into the enticing world of foraging, it is clear that our initial steps into understanding the basics of foraging merely scratch the surface of this intricate field. In this chapter, we will delve deeper, going beyond the fundamental skills we have built so far and expanding our knowledge into more specialized areas of foraging.

We will confront complex issues such as the impact of foraging on biodiversity, ethical practices, understanding complex ecosystems, and the importance of conservation. These topics will provide you with a comprehensive understanding of the ecological footprint of foraging and guide you on how to be a responsible forager.

This chapter will expose you to the potential commercial aspects of foraging, focusing on laws and regulations surrounding the sale of foraged food and the niche market that exists for these naturally abundant resources. As we consider these advanced topics, we will be transforming from amateur foragers to enlightened stewards of the land, aware of our actions' implications and committed to preserving nature's bounty for future generations.

This chapter will challenge you, incite your curiosity, and most importantly, enhance your understanding of foraging as an intricate blend of art, science, and ethics. By the end of this chapter, you will have a robust and well-rounded understanding of foraging, well-equipped to tackle the more complex issues surrounding this timeless practice.

Seasonal Foraging: What to Look for in Each Season

While the art of foraging may seem simple at first, the complexities begin to unfold when we start to consider the factor of seasonality. A successful forager must not only understand which plants are edible, but also the right time to find and harvest them. Just as the changing seasons affect the rhythms of nature, they also influence what's available in the wild to forage. Therefore, to maximize the yield and minimize the impact on nature, seasonal foraging becomes a cornerstone in the forager's knowledge base.

Spring: A Season of Rebirth and Regrowth

Spring is often considered a forager's delight. The warming temperatures and increased daylight trigger the start of plant growth, leading to an abundance of young, tender shoots and leaves. Wild asparagus and fiddlehead ferns, with their tender stalks and fronds, respectively, are prime examples of spring's bounty. Spring is also the season for foraging for early greens like nettles, dandelions, and ramps. These plants are not only delicious but also packed with nutrients, making them a valuable addition to springtime meals.

Spring also offers a variety of edible flowers, such as violets and elderflowers, which can add both flavor and aesthetics to culinary dishes. One must remember, though, these flowers are often the future fruits of these plants. Over-harvesting can reduce the fruit yields later in the season.

Summer: A Time of Abundance

As we move into summer, the landscape transforms. The lush greenery of spring makes way for a riot of colors as plants come into bloom, and fruits begin to ripen. Berries such as strawberries, raspberries, and blackberries become ready for harvest. The herbs are in full swing too, with chamomile, mint, and St. John's Wort ready to be gathered and dried for tea.

Edible weeds are plentiful and at their peak during the summer months. Purslane, Lamb's Quarters, and Pigweed are abundant in many areas and can provide a delicious and nutritious addition to salads and cooked dishes.

Autumn: The Season of Gathering

As the air starts to cool, autumn presents its own unique foraging opportunities. The star players of this season are undoubtedly mushrooms. From Chanterelles to Boletes to Hen of the Woods, many species of wild mushrooms fruit during the fall. However, mushroom foraging requires specific knowledge, as some can be poisonous or even lethal.

Aside from mushrooms, autumn is a time for nuts and seeds. Acorns, walnuts, and chestnuts can be collected and processed for a variety of culinary uses. Many fruits, like apples, pears, and persimmons, also ripen in the fall, providing a sweet treat for the diligent forager.

Winter: The Lean Season

Winter is perhaps the most challenging season for foraging, but it is not without its rewards. The bare landscape may seem devoid of edible plants, but several species can provide sustenance even in the coldest months. Evergreen trees like pines, spruces, and firs offer vitamin C-rich needles that can be made into tea. Bark and twigs from trees such as birch and willow can also be utilized in various ways.

Winter is also an excellent time to learn about tree identification through their bark and bud patterns, which can prove useful in future foraging expeditions.

In this part, we explored how each season offers its unique array of edible plants. However, it's important to note that these seasons are not distinct, and their transitions can blur based on local climate and weather patterns. Therefore, while this part provides a general guideline, foraging activities in your region may vary.

Habitat-Specific Foraging

Understanding the different environments and their unique offerings enhances a forager's knowledge and skills, allowing one to maximize their potential harvest while also preserving the integrity of each ecosystem. In this chapter, we explore ten diverse environments and the foraging opportunities they present.

Deciduous Forests: The Bounty Under the Canopy

Deciduous forests, characterized by trees that shed their leaves annually, are home to a multitude of plant species. Early springtime reveals wild garlic, ramps, and nettles, offering potent flavors and nutrients after a long winter. As summer unfolds, the forest floor and understory flourish with berries like blackberries, huckleberries, and elderberries. Autumn transforms the forest into a fungal wonderland, with mushroom species such as chanterelles, morels, and boletes appearing amidst the fallen leaves. Foragers must tread lightly, practicing sustainable harvest techniques to preserve these delicate ecosystems.

Coniferous Forests: A Unique Foraging Experience
In contrast, coniferous forests, dominated by evergreen trees, offer different foraging opportunities. Spruce and pine tips, gathered in spring, are surprisingly versatile, used in teas, seasonings, and even homemade beers. Fall presents a chance to gather pine nuts, a delicacy in many cuisines. Again, foraging in these forests requires a mindful approach, taking care not to overharvest and damage these majestic woodlands.

Meadows and Fields: The Open Pantry

Meadows and fields, with their abundant sunlight, are havens for a variety of plants. Early spring brings forth sprouts like field garlic and wild mustard greens. As summer approaches, these open spaces burst into color with wildflowers like wild roses, yarrow, and red clover, which are excellent for teas and salads. However, it's essential to forage responsibly, ensuring these areas aren't treated with harmful pesticides and respecting private properties.

Prairies: Sea of Grasses

The vast expanse of prairies offers a unique foraging environment. Here, plants such as wild asparagus, ground cherries, and prairie turnips grow, used by Native Americans for centuries. Foragers should be respectful of this ecosystem, focusing on non-endangered species and practicing sustainable harvesting methods.

Wetlands: A Water-Saturated Treasure Trove

Wetlands, including marshes, swamps, and bogs, harbor plant species adapted to water-saturated conditions. Cattails, with almost all parts edible, are an exceptional find. Watercress, marsh marigold, and wild rice also thrive in these areas. Care is necessary when foraging in wetlands to avoid waterborne pathogens and environmental pollutants.

Rivers and Streams: The Flowing Pantry

The banks of rivers and streams also present a wealth of edible plants. Watercress, wild mint, and horsetail can often be found near fresh running water. However, the purity of the water source is a crucial factor for the safety of these plants.

Coastal Areas: The Riches of the Sea

Coastal foraging offers an array of marine plants and shellfish. Sea plants like kelp, nori, and samphire are not only edible but packed with nutrients. Clams, mussels, and other shellfish can be foraged at low tide, given local regulations permit. Safety is a priority in coastal foraging, avoiding areas that may be polluted.

Alpine Areas: Foraging in High Altitudes

Higher altitudes present a unique set of edible plants. Alpine strawberries, wild thyme, and sorrel are among the hardy plants that can be found in these regions. Due to the delicate nature of these ecosystems, it's crucial to tread lightly and not disturb the landscape.

Deserts: Resilience in Arid Conditions

Deserts might seem inhospitable, but they too harbor edible species. Prickly pear cactus, mesquite pods, and certain yuccas offer sustenance amidst the sand. Foraging in these conditions requires caution and respect for the arid environment.

Urban Environments: Foraging in the Concrete Jungle

Urban foraging can yield surprising finds. Edible weeds like dandelions, plantain, and purslane commonly grow in city parks, yards, and vacant lots. Mulberry, crabapple, and other fruit trees often line city streets. It's important to forage only in areas free of pollutants and untreated with harmful chemicals.

Foraging is a way to connect with nature, no matter the landscape. Remember, each habitat has its rhythm and rules, and successful, responsible foraging respects these parameters while enjoying the bounty each season has to offer.

Foraging for Medicinal Plants and Other Useful Wild Products

Foraging extends far beyond the scope of edible plants. Nature generously offers an array of plants with medicinal properties and other useful wild products. In this section, we delve into the specifics of 10 such medicinal plants and 10 useful wild products, diving into their descriptions, benefits, habitats, and seasonality.

Medicinal Plants

1. Echinacea (Echinacea purpurea)

Description: Echinacea is a perennial plant characterized by its large, purple flowers and spiky central cone.

Benefits: Echinacea has been used traditionally to boost the immune system and fight off colds, flu, and infections.

Site: Native to North America, Echinacea is commonly found in prairies and open woodlands.

Seasonality: Echinacea flowers in mid to late summer.

2. Chamomile (Matricaria chamomilla)

Description: Chamomile is known for its delicate, daisy-like flowers and apple-like aroma.

Benefits: Chamomile is commonly used as a sleep aid and for calming anxiety. It's also used to soothe digestive issues and skin conditions.

Site: Chamomile prefers open, sunny locations and is often found in fields and along roadsides.

Seasonality: Chamomile blooms in late spring to mid-summer.

3. Peppermint (Mentha x piperita)

Description: Peppermint is a perennial plant with dark green leaves and clusters of small purple flowers.

Benefits: Peppermint is known for its digestive benefits and cooling effect. It's also used in pain relief and to relieve congestion.

Site: Peppermint is commonly found in moist habitats near streams, ditches, or other wet sites.

Seasonality: Peppermint flowers in mid to late summer.

4. Lavender (Lavandula angustifolia)

Description: Lavender is a perennial shrub known for its purple flowers and strong, distinctive scent.

Benefits: Lavender is used for stress relief, insomnia, depression, and anxiety. It also has antibacterial properties.

Site: Native to the Mediterranean, lavender prefers sunny habitats with well-drained soil.

Seasonality: Lavender blooms from late spring to early summer.

5. Milk Thistle (Silybum marianum)

Description: Milk thistle is known for its glossy, marbled leaves and tall stalks topped with purple flowers.

Benefits: Milk thistle is renowned for its liver-protective qualities. It's used to detoxify the liver and improve liver function.

Site: Milk thistle is found in Mediterranean countries, but has been introduced to other parts of the world, often in disturbed areas.

Seasonality: Milk thistle flowers in late spring to early summer.

Useful Wild Products

1. Pine (Pinus)

Description: Pine is a type of coniferous tree characterized by long, needle-like leaves.

Benefits: Pine needles are high in vitamin C and can be used to make a nutritious tea. Pine sap can also be used as a natural adhesive or waterproofing agent.

Site: Pines are found in various habitats from mountainous regions to flat wetlands, thriving in well-drained soil.

Seasonality: Pine needles can be collected year-round, while the sap flows most freely in late winter and spring.

2. Cattail (Typha)

Description: Cattails are tall, perennial plants known for their distinctive, cigar-shaped flower heads.

Benefits: The fluff from mature cattail flowers makes excellent tinder for fire-starting. The stalks can be used for weaving mats or baskets.

Site: Cattails are found in wetlands around the world.

Seasonality: Cattail fluff is typically collected in late summer or early autumn when the flower heads mature.

3. Willow (Salix)

Description: Willows are deciduous trees or shrubs known for their long, flexible branches.

Benefits: Willow branches are excellent for weaving into baskets, furniture, and other useful items. The bark contains salicin, a natural pain reliever.

Site: Willows are found in moist soil along rivers, lakes, and other water bodies across temperate regions.

Seasonality: Willow branches can be harvested year-round, but they are most flexible in the spring.

4. Birch (Betula)

Description: Birch is a type of deciduous tree known for its distinctive, white bark.

Benefits: Birch bark is waterproof and can be used to make containers or to start fires. Birch sap can be tapped and drunk fresh or fermented into birch sap wine.

Site: Birches are found in temperate and boreal climates, often in open, sunny areas with well-drained soil.

Seasonality: Birch sap is usually tapped in the early spring when the sap begins to flow.

5. Nettle (Urtica dioica)

Description: Nettle is a perennial plant characterized by its dark green, serrated leaves covered in tiny, stinging hairs.

Benefits: Nettle fibers can be used to make strong, durable cordage. Nettle leaves are also highly nutritious and can be cooked and eaten or made into tea.

Site: Nettles are found in rich soil in forests, fields, and along waterways.

Seasonality: Nettle fibers are typically harvested in the autumn after the plant has gone to seed.

In conclusion, the world of foraging opens up a treasure trove of resources beyond food. From medicinal plants with healing properties to versatile wild products, nature offers a multitude of gifts that require only knowledge and respect for the environment to utilize effectively.

From understanding the seasonal shifts of nature and knowing what to look for in each season, we've acquired the knowledge to maximize our foraging yield all year round. We've also gained insights into how to adjust our foraging strategies to different environments, enabling us to effectively forage in forests, meadows, coastal areas, urban environments, and more.

Moreover, we've explored the rich realm of medicinal plants and other useful wild products, learning about their unique properties, benefits, and uses. This deeper understanding of the valuable resources that nature provides paves the way for us to make the most of our foraging adventures.

As we've seen throughout this chapter, advanced foraging requires knowledge, respect for nature, and an understanding of the intricate connections within ecosystems. Equipped with these tools, we can venture out into the wild with confidence, knowing we're capable of sourcing a variety of edibles, medicinal plants, and other useful products responsibly and sustainably.

Whether you're seeking food, medicine, or practical materials, the world of foraging is boundlessly rewarding.

Chapter 8
Foraging Journeys: Real-Life Stories

In the vast panorama of nature, a single step can lead us into a world of abundance and wonder. The world of foraging is a realm where knowledge, skill, and respect for the environment combine, taking us back to our ancient roots and connecting us more deeply with the earth. It's a journey of discovery, of learning, and of building relationships - not just with the plants and the land, but also with ourselves and our communities. In this chapter, we delve into the personal side of foraging, sharing the unique experiences, valuable lessons learned, and the profound impacts this journey can have on our lives.

In the preceding chapters, we have navigated through the technicalities, practices, and intricate details of foraging. Now, it's time to step back and view the big picture, understanding how these aspects come together to form the rich tapestry of the foraging experience. This chapter offers a behind-the-scenes look at the adventure of foraging - the trials and triumphs, the unexpected discoveries, and the lessons learned along the way.

From the first ventures into the wilderness to the continued exploration of known and new terrains, we'll recount the experiences that have shaped the journey, reflecting on how they have informed and refined the practice of foraging. We will share personal stories of memorable foraging expeditions, the joy of discovering new edibles, the wisdom gleaned from mistakes, and the rewards of persevering through challenges.

This chapter is also a testament to the transformative power of foraging. It's not just about the physical act of gathering food or other materials from the wild - it's also about how this simple act can profoundly shape our perspectives, our relationships with the natural world, and our understanding of our place within it.

As we traverse through these stories, we hope they inspire you, provide insights into the realities of foraging, and perhaps, spark in you the spirit of exploration and a deep appreciation for the gifts of nature. Welcome to the personal side of the foraging journey.

My Foraging Journey: Personal Experiences and Lessons Learned

Embarking on the foraging journey was no sudden leap, but a slow, intuitive progression towards a more holistic understanding and experience of the natural world around me. Like a delicate fern unfurling its fronds towards the sunlight, my interest in foraging developed organically. It was a gradual process of opening my senses and my heart to the incredible bounty and wisdom that nature offers.

Early in life, my connection with the outdoors was mainly recreational. Nature was a place for camping trips, hikes, and picnics, a respite from the bustle of city life. But then, I started to look at the landscape differently. It was no longer just a backdrop for outdoor activities, but a complex, interconnected system that was teeming with life and resources. My initial forays into foraging were hesitant and exploratory, guided more by curiosity than any concrete knowledge.

One of the first wild edibles I successfully identified and consumed was the dandelion. To most people, it was a mere weed, an unwelcome invader in their manicured lawns. To me, it became a symbol of my nascent foraging journey. I was fascinated by the versatility of this plant – from the bright yellow flowers to the jagged green leaves and the long taproot, every part of the dandelion had something to offer. And it was right there, in my backyard!

As my knowledge about wild edibles expanded, so did my palate. I ventured into forests and fields, creek sides and meadows, gathering nettles, chickweed, morels, and more. Each edible plant had a unique taste, a unique texture – a character of its own. But more than the physical nourishment they provided, foraging fed something deeper within me. It was a way to connect with the cycles of the seasons, the rhythms of the natural world.

Of course, the journey was not always smooth. For every successful forage, there were instances of misidentification and near-misses with toxic lookalikes. I remember once confusing the benign plantain with the poisonous foxglove. I was about to sample a leaf when a fellow forager pointed out my mistake. That incident served as a stark reminder of the importance of thorough research, cautious identification, and the practice of never consuming anything unless I was entirely sure of its identity.

The art of foraging, I came to understand, was not merely about collecting food, but about building a relationship with the land. It was about learning to read the language of the landscape – recognizing the signs of fertile soil, understanding how the presence of one plant could indicate the likelihood of others, predicting the ripening of berries based on temperature and rainfall patterns.

One of the most rewarding experiences of my foraging journey was coming across a patch of wild asparagus. I had been studying the plants for weeks, observing their growth, waiting for the perfect moment to harvest. When the time was right, I returned to the patch, armed with a knife and a basket. Cutting through the spears, feeling their fresh, crisp texture, I was struck by a profound sense of gratitude. Here was a gift from nature, a product of the earth's generosity. I was merely the receiver.

Foraging has transformed not just my relationship with nature, but also with food. I've come to appreciate the hard work and dedication that goes into growing and harvesting the food we eat. I've become more aware of the environmental impacts of our food choices and more committed to sustainable practices.

My foraging journey has had its share of mistakes, risks, and surprises. But it's these experiences that have enriched the journey, making it not just about the destination (the food on my plate), but also about the path taken, the knowledge gained, and the connections forged. From my first dandelion to the latest mushroom hunt, every step of the way has been a lesson in humility, patience, respect, and gratitude.

In sharing my personal experiences, I hope to convey that foraging is more than a skill or a hobby. It's a way of life, an ongoing dialogue with the natural world. It's an adventure that invites us to slow down, observe, learn, and ultimately, appreciate the intricate, beautiful, and generous systems of nature that sustain us. The foraging journey is an incredible one, filled with invaluable lessons and experiences. So, here's to the journey, the discoveries, and the wild flavors that await.

Voices from the Field: Interviews with Experienced Foragers

Having explored my personal journey with foraging, let's turn our attention to the insights and experiences of fellow foragers who have also ventured into this unique world of wild edibles. In this section, we will take a look at the invaluable knowledge and fascinating experiences shared by these seasoned foragers, each of them having their unique perspective and methodology that contributes to a richer understanding of the art of foraging.

Interview with Jane Thompson:

Jane Thompson, a retired botanist with more than two decades of foraging experience, shares her perspective on the importance of understanding plant biology for successful foraging. She emphasizes the interconnection between plants and their environment, stressing that "Each plant has its own story to tell. It's crucial to understand the plant's lifecycle, its preferred habitat, and its seasonal variations. This knowledge can turn an aimless walk into a fruitful forage."

Jane's favorite foraged food? Wild ramps. "Ramps have a delicate, sweet flavor unlike anything you'd find in the grocery store. I only take what I need and make sure to leave plenty for the plant to continue its growth and reproduction."

Interview with Martin Baxter:

Martin Baxter, an avid outdoorsman and foraging instructor, reflects on the role of respect and sustainability in foraging. "To me, foraging is not just about taking from the land. It's about giving back, too. I always remind my students to forage sustainably. It's not just for us, it's for the animals, the insects, the entire ecosystem."

Martin's advice to novice foragers? "Start with one or two plants, learn them really well. Know how to identify them in all stages of growth. Know where they grow. Know their seasons. This will give you confidence and make your foraging safer and more productive."

Interview with Maya Ramirez:

Maya Ramirez, a professional chef with a passion for wild foods, talks about the unique flavors that wild edibles can bring to the table. "Wild foods have flavors that you can't find in cultivated plants. Like the tartness of sorrel, the pepperiness of watercress, or the earthiness of wild mushrooms. These flavors can really elevate a dish."

Maya's favorite recipe involving foraged foods? "Nettle soup. It's simple, nutritious, and utterly delicious. The nettles have a mild, sweet flavor that's just wonderful. But remember to wear gloves when you're picking them!"

Interview with Tom Schneider:

Tom Schneider, a biologist and foraging guide, speaks about the importance of safety and proper identification. "One wrong identification can lead to serious consequences. But don't let this scare you. The key is to take your time, study carefully, and when in doubt, don't eat."

Tom's most exciting foraging find? "Finding a stand of wild pawpaw trees was incredible. The fruits are delicious, like a cross between banana, mango, and melon. But it was the discovery, the joy of finding something unexpected, that was the real thrill."

Interview with Lisa Collins:

Lisa Collins, a mother who loves to forage with her children, highlights the importance of passing on the knowledge to the younger generation. "It's such a joy to see my kids connecting with nature, learning about plants, understanding where their food comes from. They're developing respect for the environment and gaining practical skills."

Lisa's go-to foraged food for the family? "Wild berries. The kids love them. We pick them in the summer, make jam, freeze some for the winter. It's a wonderful family activity and the results are delicious."

Through these interviews, we get a glimpse into the diverse world of foraging. Each of these experienced foragers brings their unique approach, demonstrating that there are many ways to engage in and enjoy this practice. They also underscore the importance of respect, knowledge, safety, and sustainability, values that are central to the practice of foraging. These stories offer inspiration, practical advice, and a shared sense of connection with nature that resonates with anyone embarking on the journey of foraging.

Chapter 9
Resources and Further Learning

The journey into the world of foraging is a rewarding and continuous learning experience. There is always a new plant to discover, a different technique to master, or an intriguing bit of folklore to unravel. This chapter is designed to provide you with the necessary tools and resources to continue your learning journey even beyond this book.

Every forager, whether novice or seasoned, recognizes the importance of reliable and accessible resources to guide their exploration of wild edibles. From field guides and botanical references to online forums and educational courses, there are countless resources available that cater to different learning styles and preferences. In this chapter, we will delve into these resources, providing you with a comprehensive list of books, websites, apps, courses, and communities that can serve as your roadmap in the ever-expanding landscape of foraging.

Foraging is not just about recognizing and gathering edible plants. It's about building a deep understanding and respect for the ecosystems that we are part of. It's about connecting with our ancestral roots and embracing the rhythms of nature. It's about nurturing our curiosity and wonder as we explore the world around us. And most importantly, it's about sharing the knowledge we acquire and contributing to the sustainable practices that protect and preserve our natural world for generations to come.

Continuing education and resourcefulness are fundamental to the foraging journey. These resources we'll discuss are not meant to replace the practical and experiential knowledge contained within this book but to supplement and expand upon it. The knowledge we acquire is a stepping stone, and these resources are bridges to broader understanding and skills.

This chapter will help you build a foundation for further exploration and learning. By understanding the resources at your disposal, you can navigate your foraging journey with greater confidence and enrich your experiences in the wild. Remember, the art of foraging is an ongoing journey of discovery, and the landscape of knowledge is vast and ever-changing. With curiosity as your compass and these resources as your guide, the world of foraging is yours to explore.

Expanding Your Knowledge

With a world that's constantly evolving and an ecosystem that's as dynamic as it is diverse, the pursuit of knowledge in the realm of foraging is ongoing. There's always something new to learn, an unfamiliar plant species to discover, or a fresh perspective to understand. So, in this section, we'll explore a selection of books, websites, and courses, each resource a treasure trove of wisdom for foragers seeking to expand their knowledge and expertise.

Books

Books are an indispensable resource for any forager. The tactile sensation of flipping through a field guide while out on a forage, the ability to pore over botanical illustrations in the quiet of the evening, or the pleasure of immersing oneself in the wealth of knowledge contained within their pages make them an essential part of a forager's arsenal. Here are some recommendations:

1.   "The Forager's Harvest: A Guide to Identifying, Harvesting, and Preparing Edible Wild Plants" by Samuel Thayer - A comprehensive guide, Thayer's book is lauded for its accuracy and in-depth descriptions of various edible plants found in North America.

2.   "Nature's Garden: A Guide to Identifying, Harvesting, and Preparing Wild Edible Plants" by Samuel Thayer – This is another gem by Thayer and is a perfect companion to his first book, delving deeper into foraging methodologies and providing extensive profiles of wild edibles.

3.   "Wild Edibles: A Practical Guide to Foraging" by Sergei Boutenko – This book is excellent for beginners, offering clear guidance on safe foraging practices, identification tips, and includes recipes for turning your foraged finds into delicious meals.

4.   "The Wild Wisdom of Weeds" by Katrina Blair – An interesting read that focuses on the edible and medicinal properties of 13 of the world's most common weeds.

Websites

In this digital age, countless websites provide a vast array of information for foragers. Here are a few that stand out:

1.   "Forager's Harvest" (**www.foragersharvest.com**) - Samuel Thayer's website, an extension of his popular books, offers excellent information on edible plants.

2.   "Eat The Weeds" (**www.eattheweeds.com**) - Managed by Green Deane, this website is a valuable source for information about edible wild plants, and features a wide array of plants with detailed descriptions.

3.   "Wild Food UK" (**www.wildfooduk.com**) - This is a great resource for those based in the UK. The website has a vast database of British wild edibles and offers foraging courses as well.

Courses

Attending a foraging course can significantly enhance your skills, offering hands-on experience under the guidance of experts. Here are some recommended courses:

1.   "The Herbal Academy's Botany and Wildcrafting Course" – This course offers an in-depth exploration of plant identification and wildcrafting.

2.   "Online Foraging Course" by "Wild Food UK" – This comprehensive online course covers a range of UK edible plants, mushrooms, and seaweeds.

3.   "Foraging and Feasting: A Field Guide and Wild Food Cookbook" by Dina Falconi – Not only is this a course, but it's also a beautiful field guide and cookbook.

These resources offer a wealth of knowledge that can enhance your understanding and hone your skills in foraging. However, it's crucial to remember that while these tools provide valuable information, the best teacher is often the natural world itself. So take these resources with you as you step outdoors, but never forget to listen to the whispers of the wild around you. Therein lies the greatest wisdom.

Community Connections: Local Foraging Groups and Classes

Foraging, while it can be a solitary pursuit, is often enriched by the shared experiences and collective knowledge that come from being part of a community. Whether you're a novice forager seeking guidance or an experienced one looking to share your expertise, becoming involved in local foraging groups and classes can be immensely beneficial. These platforms provide opportunities for learning, sharing, and forging connections with like-minded individuals.

Local Foraging Groups

Local foraging groups are communities bound by a shared interest in wild foods. These groups regularly organize foraging excursions, where experienced foragers guide novices in identifying, harvesting, and preparing wild foods. The collaborative spirit of these outings enables members to learn from each other, share knowledge, and experience the thrill of discovery together.

One such group is the 'Forage London' in the UK. Led by experienced forager John Rensten, the group organizes frequent foraging walks around London and the South East. They explore a wide range of habitats, from urban parks to coastal regions, demonstrating that bountiful foraging opportunities can be found even in the most unexpected places.

In the United States, the 'Mushroom Club of Georgia' serves as a platform for mycology enthusiasts to come together. They hold regular mushroom forays, provide education on mushroom identification, and promote the conservation of fungi.

Local Foraging Classes

Local foraging classes are another way to connect with the foraging community. These classes, often led by seasoned foragers, offer structured learning opportunities and hands-on experience in identifying and harvesting wild foods.

The 'Wild Food School' in Cornwall, UK, offers one such opportunity. Founded by Marcus Harrison, a forager with over 30 years of experience, the school offers courses that cover various aspects of foraging. These include plant identification, safe and sustainable harvesting practices, and the preparation of foraged foods.

In North America, the 'Wild Abundance' school in Asheville, North Carolina, offers a variety of classes and workshops, including their popular 'Wild Edibles Foraging Adventure'. This class not only teaches participants about the plethora of edible plants in the region but also guides them on how to sustainably harvest and prepare these wild foods.

Connecting with the local foraging community through groups and classes is a rewarding way to deepen your knowledge and appreciation of foraging. However, the true value of these communities lies in the shared experiences, the joy of discovery, and the connections forged with fellow foragers and the natural world.

Whether you join a group or attend a class, the essence of foraging is encapsulated in the journey - the exploration of the wild, the thrill of the find, and the delight of sharing and learning in the company of others. These experiences imbue foraging with a sense of community, transforming it from a solitary pursuit into a shared adventure. So step out, connect, and let the world of foraging unfold before you.

Citizen Science and Conservation Opportunities for Foragers

One of the most rewarding aspects of foraging is the intimate connection it fosters with the natural world. As foragers, we are not only beneficiaries of nature's bounty but also its stewards. Our understanding and appreciation of our local ecosystems make us ideally suited to play a role in their preservation and conservation. This section explores how foragers can give back to nature through citizen science initiatives and conservation opportunities.

Citizen science projects are a way for the public to contribute to scientific research. These projects tap into the power of collective observation, inviting individuals to contribute data from their local environments. Foragers, with their keen observational skills and knowledge of local flora, are perfect candidates for such initiatives.

For example, Project BudBurst is a national citizen science campaign in the United States. It encourages people to observe and record phenological events - the timing of leafing, flowering, and fruiting - in their local environment. Data contributed by volunteers help scientists to track shifts in these events due to climate change. Foragers, who are often already attuned to these seasonal changes due to their foraging activities, can make valuable contributions to such initiatives.

Another initiative is the Great Sunflower Project. Participants grow sunflowers, then monitor and record the frequency of pollinator visits. This data helps scientists understand the challenges faced by bees and other pollinators. As foragers, understanding the integral role these pollinators play in maintaining the plants we rely on for food makes participation in such projects both valuable and fulfilling.

Beyond citizen science, there are numerous conservation opportunities available to foragers. Conservation organizations often need volunteers for activities such as native plant restoration, invasive species removal, and habitat conservation. In the UK, the Wildlife Trusts run various local projects where volunteers can get involved in conserving their local wildlife habitats.

In the United States, organizations like the Nature Conservancy offer similar volunteer opportunities. For instance, they run an Adopt an Acre program, where individuals can contribute to the protection and management of critical ecosystems. Such activities not only help protect the environment but also ensure the sustainability of foraging practices.

In conclusion, foragers are in a unique position to contribute to citizen science initiatives and conservation efforts. By participating in these activities, foragers can give back to the ecosystems they depend on, ensuring their health and vitality for future generations. They can also help bridge the gap between scientists and the public, fostering a broader understanding and appreciation of our natural world. It is a way for the foraging community to turn their passion for wild foods into a force for good, amplifying the benefits of foraging beyond the dinner plate and into the wider world.

Appendix

Glossary of Foraging and Botanical Terms

Annual: A type of plant that completes its entire lifecycle, from seed to flower to seed again, within a single year or growing season.

Basal rosette: A circular arrangement of leaves, or other plant structures, at the base of the plant stem at ground level.

Biennial: A type of plant that takes two years to complete its life cycle. In the first year, the plant grows leaves, stems, and roots, and then it enters a period of dormancy over the colder months. In the second year, the plant blooms and develops seeds before dying.

Composite flower: A flower head that is composed of many smaller flowers. The individual flowers, called florets, are arranged in a tight cluster that appears to be a single flower.

Deciduous: A term used to describe trees or shrubs that shed their leaves annually, typically in the autumn.

Evergreen: A term used to describe trees or shrubs that retain their leaves throughout the year.

Foraging: The act of searching for and gathering food resources in the wild.

Habitat: The natural environment in which a plant or animal lives. This could be a forest, meadow, wetland, desert, or any other natural ecosystem.

Perennial: A type of plant that lives for more than two years. It produces flowers and seeds over a long time.

Rhizome: A type of underground stem that sends out roots and shoots from its nodes. Some plants propagate through rhizomes.

Rosette: A circular arrangement of leaves or petals. In plants, it often refers to leaves emerging from the stem at ground level in a circular pattern.

Stem: The main structural part of a plant that provides support and transports water, nutrients, and sugars between the roots and leaves.

Venation: The pattern of veins in a leaf or an insect's wing. In leaves, these veins can provide valuable clues for plant identification.

Wildcrafting: The practice of harvesting plants from their natural or "wild" habitat, for food, medicinal, or other purposes. It is similar to foraging but typically implies a focus on sustainable and ethical harvesting practices to conserve and support the ecosystem.

This glossary should help to clarify some of the specific terms used throughout this book. Understanding these terms will enrich your foraging experience and give you the language needed to engage with other foragers, botanists, and naturalists.

Quick Identification Guide

When starting your journey into foraging, being able to correctly and confidently identify common edible plants is key. This quick identification guide provides you with an overview of these plants, their key identifying features, and their common habitats.

Please note, that foraging requires careful identification of each plant. Misidentification can lead to consuming toxic plants. Always cross-reference multiple resources and when in doubt, don't consume.

Dandelion (Taraxacum officinale):

Dandelion is an extremely common edible plant identifiable by its bright yellow flowers, deeply toothed leaves arranged in a rosette at the base of the plant, and hollow stem. When the flower matures, it turns into a round ball of white, fluffy seeds that can be blown away with the wind. This plant can be found in a variety of habitats such as lawns, roadsides, and other disturbed areas.

Purslane (Portulaca oleracea):

Purslane is a succulent-like plant with red-tinted stems and thick, fleshy, paddle-shaped leaves that are often clustered together. In the summer, it produces yellow flowers. Purslane is typically found in sunny, well-drained areas, such as gardens, fields, and sidewalk cracks.

Wood Sorrel (Oxalis spp.):

Wood Sorrel is identifiable by its clover-like appearance, but unlike clover, its leaves are heart-shaped and appear in sets of three. The leaves are often folded along the center vein. The flowers are delicate and can be white, pink, or yellow depending on the species. Wood Sorrel is typically found in shaded areas, such as forests and hedgerows

Nettle (Urtica dioica):

Nettle is a tall, perennial plant known for its stinging hairs on the leaves and stems. The leaves are toothed, pointed, and arranged oppositely on the stem. Nettle prefers rich, moist soils and is often found in forests, along rivers, or in disturbed areas.

Wild Garlic (Allium ursinum):

Wild Garlic, also known as ramsons or bear's garlic, has long, pointed leaves that are similar to the leaves of lilies of the valley. However, it can be distinguished by its strong garlic smell. In the spring, it produces clusters of white, star-shaped flowers. Wild Garlic typically grows in damp, shady woods.

Chickweed (Stellaria media):

Chickweed is a low-growing plant that can form dense mats. It has small, pointed leaves and tiny, white, star-like flowers. A key feature is a single line of hairs along the stem. Chickweed prefers cool, moist areas, and it's commonly found in gardens and fields.

Plantain (Plantago spp.):

Plantain, not to be confused with the tropical fruit, has broad or lance-shaped leaves that emerge from a basal rosette, and tall, slender flower spikes. The leaves have parallel veins. Plantain can be found in many habitats, including lawns, fields, roadsides, and other disturbed areas.

Elderberry (Sambucus nigra):

Elderberry is a shrub or small tree known for its clusters of small, white flowers and small, dark purple berries. The plant has compound leaves with 5 to 7 leaflets. Elderberry is commonly found in both wet and dry habitats, such as forests, hedgerows, and roadsides.

Burdock (Arctium lappa):

Burdock is a biennial plant recognizable by its large, heart-shaped leaves and round, bur-like flower heads. It's most known for its deep, fleshy roots. It typically grows in disturbed areas, along roadsides, and at the edges of fields.

Yarrow (Achillea millefolium):

Yarrow is a perennial herb identifiable by its feathery leaves and clusters of small, white or pink flowers. Yarrow can be found in a variety of habitats, such as meadows, fields, and roadsides.

Mullein (Verbascum thapsus):

Mullein is a biennial plant known for its rosette of large, fuzzy leaves in the first year, and a tall, yellow flower spike in the second year. Mullein prefers sunny, disturbed areas, and is often found along roadsides and in pastures.

Stinging Nettle (Urtica dioica):

Stinging Nettle is a perennial plant recognized by its heart-shaped, toothed leaves, and tiny, greenish or white flowers. The entire plant is covered with tiny, stinging hairs. Stinging Nettle prefers rich, moist soil, and is often found along streams or in disturbed areas.

Blackberry (Rubus fruticosus):

Blackberry is a thorny shrub or vine known for its compound leaves with three to five leaflets and clusters of small, white to pink flowers. The plant produces familiar blackberry fruits. Blackberries are commonly found in forests, fields, and disturbed areas.

Wild Strawberry (Fragaria vesca):

Wild Strawberry is a low-growing plant recognizable by its trifoliate leaves and small, white flowers. The plant produces small, red strawberries. Wild Strawberry prefers sunny areas and is often found in fields, forests, and roadsides.

Common Nettle (Urtica dioica):

Despite its sting, when cooked, the nettle is a great source of vitamins and minerals.

Lamb's Quarters (Chenopodium album):

Often considered a weed, the young leaves can be used much like spinach.

Mulberry (Morus spp.):

The fruit from this tree is very tasty and can be eaten directly or used in pies, wines, and cordials.

Wild Raspberry (Rubus idaeus):

Found in a variety of habitats, the berries are deliciously sweet when ripe.

Juniper (Juniperus spp.):

The berries are used as a spice and in flavoring gin.

Elderberry (Sambucus nigra):

The flowers and ripe berries are edible; however, all other parts of the plant are poisonous.

Hickory (Carya spp.):

The nuts from this tree are a valuable source of food.

Watercress (Nasturtium officinale):

Found in running water, watercress leaves have a spicy flavor.

Jerusalem Artichoke (Helianthus tuberosus):

The tubers can be eaten raw or cooked.

Borage (Borago officinalis):

The flowers and leaves are edible and have a mild cucumber flavor.

Evening Primrose (Oenothera biennis):

The root can be eaten as a vegetable, and the young seedpods can be cooked.

Chicory (Cichorium intybus):

The leaves and flowers can be eaten in salads, and the roots can be roasted to make a coffee substitute

Sheep Sorrel (Rumex acetosella):

The leaves have a tangy taste and can be added to salads.

Serviceberry (Amelanchier spp.):

Also known as Juneberry, the fruits are delicious and can be eaten raw or used in baking.

Teaberry (Gaultheria procumbens):

Also known as wintergreen, the berries and leaves, when steeped in hot water, make a flavorful tea.

Burdock (Arctium lappa):

The root can be used as a root vegetable and is very sweet.

Daylily (Hemerocallis fulva):

The flowers and buds are edible and can be used in a variety of dishes.

Garlic Mustard (Alliaria petiolata):

Both the leaves and the seeds can be used in cooking.

Kudzu (Pueraria montana):

Often considered an invasive species, the leaves, shoots, blossoms, and roots are all edible.

Seasonal Foraging Calendar:

The ever-changing cycle of seasons imparts a pulsating rhythm to the natural world. As the earth revolves around the sun, life on earth orchestrates its progression in a symphony of growth, blossoming, fruiting, and dormancy. This ceaseless dance of nature translates to a perpetual buffet of wild foods that shift with the ebb and flow of seasons. From the sprouting greens of spring to the abundant fruits of summer, the nutty bounty of fall, and the resilient offerings of winter, each season presents unique foraging opportunities. In this section, we shall journey through the calendar, marking the seasonal availability of various forageable species.

January:

Winter may seem devoid of life, but careful observation reveals a plethora of edible species. Look for resilient wintergreens such as chickweed and bittercress or tap into the energy reserves of trees by learning to identify and safely harvest tree barks such as slippery elm. Another plant, the stinging nettle, offers nourishing young shoots, which are best when cooked.

February:

As winter gradually loses its grip, some early bloomers like the dandelion and garlic mustard can be seen. Late in February, you can often find budding trees like maples and birches, from which sap can be collected and boiled down to a delicious syrup.

March:

The warming temperatures of March coax out the early spring greens. Species like wild leek, fiddlehead ferns, and ramps become available for the taking. Wood sorrel, with its characteristic lemony tang, can also be found.

April:

April continues the trend of abundant spring greens. Morel mushrooms begin to appear, a favorite amongst foragers for their distinctive flavor. Stinging nettles are at their peak, and wild violets begin to blossom.

May:

May is a time of floral bounty. Trees like black locust and linden offer edible flowers. Elderflowers come into bloom, and honeysuckle blossoms can be found as well. For the fungi foragers, late May often sees the emergence of oyster mushrooms.

June:

As summer sets in, the season of berries begins. Look for strawberries in early June, followed by mulberries and then raspberries. June is also when the elderberries start to ripen.

July:

The berry season continues in full swing, with blueberries and blackberries joining the fray. July also marks the start of the wild plum season. For those near the coast, it's also the perfect time for beach foraging with coastal plants like sea beet and samphire being abundant.

August:

In August, the berry season concludes with blackberries at their ripest. Many tree fruits, such as wild apples, pears, and peaches, become ready for harvest. Nuts like hazelnuts begin to ripen, and wild grapes sweeten.

September:

As summer gives way to fall, September brings a mushroom bonanza. Chanterelles, porcini, and hen-of-the-woods mushrooms can be found. Acorns, hickory nuts, and walnuts drop, adding a crunchy delight to the foraging basket.

October:

October brings a continuation of the mushroom and nut harvest. Rose hips ripen, offering a vitamin C-rich food source. This is also the time when crabapples and quinces are at their best.

November:

As the leaves fall, November offers the last flush of edible mushrooms like oyster and shaggy mane. Root vegetables such as wild parsnip, Jerusalem artichoke, and burdock can be dug up.

December:

With the onset of winter, look for wintergreens such as chickweed, watercress, and field mustard. The roots of evening primrose can be dug up and cooked, and the seeds of nettle and yellow dock can be harvested.

This guide serves as a general overview, and foraging can greatly depend on regional and yearly variations in climate. Foraging requires a blend of knowledge, observation, and respect for nature. So arm yourself with a good field guide, tread lightly, and let the seasons guide your foraging journey.

Made in the USA
Las Vegas, NV
30 October 2023

79934348R10072